Religious Politics
in Latin America,
Pentecostal vs.
Catholic

Religious Politics in Latin America, Pentecostal vs. Catholic

Brian H. Smith

University of Notre Dame Press
Notre Dame, Indiana

Library of Congress Cataloging-in-Publication Data
Smith, Brian H., 1940-
    Religious politics in Latin America, Pentecostal vs. Catholic/
Brian H. Smith.
        p. cm. — (A title from the Helen Kellogg Institute for
International Studies)
    Includes bibliographical references and index.
    ISBN 0-268-01662-3 (pbk. : alk. paper)
    1. Latin America—Church history—20th century.
2. Pentecostals—Latin America—History. 3. Catholic
Church—Latin America—History—20th century.
4. Pentecostals—Relations—Catholic Church—History.
5. Catholic Church—Relations—Pentecostals—History—
20th century. I. Title. II. Series.
BR600.S65   1998
278'.082—dc21   97-46842

CONTENTS

ACKNOWLEDGMENTS

This research was supported by a 1995 Summer Stipend from the National Endowment for the Humanities (NEH) for which I am most grateful.

I would also like to acknowledge the invaluable assistance of Professor Andrew J. Stein of the Political Science Department at Tennessee Technological University. From the very beginning of the project Andrew provided me with several extremely helpful bibliographical materials and references as well as some excellent constructive criticisms on the first draft of this manuscript.

Reverend Edward L. Cleary, O.P., of the Political Science Department of Providence College read the manuscript twice and also gave me several suggestions on how to strengthen it and bring it up to date for publication after the first draft was completed in 1995. I owe him many thanks for his encouragement in completing this work and for his warm colleagueship along the way.

Professor Michael Fleet of the Political Science Department of Marquette University also acted as constructive critic and supportive colleague during the writing of this book.

My family—Mary Kaye, Sean, and Katie—showed great patience with me during the peculiarly hot Wisconsin summer of 1995 and let me "hide out" in the cool basement until the opus was done.

1

PENTECOSTAL EXPANSION, CATHOLIC RETRENCHMENT

One of the most significant cultural changes in Latin America in the past two generations has been the steady growth of Protestantism in a region that has traditionally been overwhelmingly Catholic for 500 years. The expansion has been so significant that some estimates are by the middle of the next century Protestants may outnumber Catholics in Latin America. Moreover, the vast majority of these converts are among the poorest classes and affiliated with fundamentalist branches of Protestantism, particularly those with a Pentecostal character.

At the same time that Protestantism has been growing steadily, Catholicism has been experiencing some serious internal tensions following intense social and political commitments in the 1960s and 1970s. Clerical involvement in partisan politics, Catholic collaboration in Marxist parties and movements, and episcopal calls for substantial structural reforms favoring the poor all have created serious divisions among Catholics and raised concerns in Rome about a severely politicized Church. In order to restore unity in the Catholic Church, and to make it more competitive with Protestantism, the Vatican has been insisting that greater emphasis be given to spiritual rather than political issues and to obedience to church authority.

The focus of this book will be to review the literature on the reasons for Pentecostal growth and Catholic retrenchment, as well as assess the socioeconomic and political implications of these religious changes for democratic governments in the hemisphere, many of which follow upon a decade or more of military rule in their respective societies.

Dramatic Expansion of Pentecostalism in Latin America

Since the middle of the nineteenth century there has been a Protestant presence in Latin America due to European immigration (especially from England and Germany) and U.S. mission activity (accelerated after the Spanish-American War of 1898). These denominations transplanted from the North Atlantic region were primarily mainline Protestant churches, including Lutherans, Presbyterians, Anglicans, Episcopalians, Methodists, and Baptists. After a century of proselytization these churches, however, still only constituted about 1 percent of the overall population in the 1950s. (Latourette 1961, 300–303; 1962, 168–70; Bastian 1992, 330).

Since the 1950s, however, evangelical forms of Christianity, especially Pentecostalism (present in small numbers since the turn of the century), have been growing very rapidly. The result is that Protestantism by the early 1990s had over 50 million followers (approximately 11 percent of the population in Latin America), with Pentecostal denominations accounting for between one-half and three-quarters of their present number (D. Martin 1990, 50; Miller 191). Currently, in fact, Pentecostals account for between 75 and 90 percent of all Protestant growth in Latin America (Cleary 1997, 4). Approximately 8,000 to 10,000 people are converting to these new churches throughout Latin America every day (Goonan 1996, 3).

In some countries, where the growth of Pentecostalism has been the most dramatic, the portion of Protestants in the population is much higher. By the early 1990s it had reached 20 percent in Guatemala, Nicaragua, and Brazil, for example (Wilson 1997, 145; Goonan 1996, 3). On an average Sunday, in fact, there may be more Protestants attending church than Catholics in many Latin American countries (Stewart-Gambino 1994, 133).

In Brazil—the nation with the largest number of baptized Catholics in the world (116 million)—by 1985 there were over 15,000 Protestant ministers compared to only 13,176 Catholic priests (D. Martin 1990, 50–51; Stoll 1990, 333–34). Between 1992 and 1994 approximately 300,000 residents in Rio de Janeiro left the Catholic Church to join Protestant congregations (overwhelmingly those with a Pentecostal character) so that by the mid-1990s there were over 25 million Protestants in the country (Tautz 1996).

Although it is always tentative to extrapolate on the basis of current trends which may change, if these growth rates continue it is estimated that by the year 2010 about one of every three Latin Americans may be Protestant (Goonan 1996, 3; Stoll 1990, 337–38).

Pentecostalism differs from the historic Protestant churches in several important ways. Theologically, there is a strong emphasis on the literal nature of truth in the Bible, on the importance of experiencing the Holy Spirit in one's life (personal conversion encounters with Jesus Christ, strong, identifiable experiences of the Lord in one's life, physical and spiritual healings, speaking in tongues), and on missionary commitment by each member to spread the faith. Organizationally, these churches are much more decentralized than historic Protestant denominations, with little or no hierarchy above the local pastor, and they often do not require any academic training for their ministers (Stoll 1990, 3–4; Cleary 1997, 7–10). Sociologically, unlike the historic Protestant churches that have appealed primarily to the middle classes, Pentecostalism in Latin America has grown most dramatically among urban and rural workers (Deiros 1991, 160–62; Galindo 1992, 155–64; 269–93).[1]

Explanations for Pentecostal Growth

There have been various explanations given for the increase in Latin American Protestantism since the 1950s. Some have attributed it to forces external to Latin America (increased foreign missionary activity, U.S. economic and political penetration), or socioeconomic changes in Latin America itself (breakdown of traditional agrarian structures, growth of industrialization, migration, and social uprootedness). Still others point to the failures of Catholicism (chronic scarcity of priests, traditional identification with upper-class elites, formalistic rituals, clerical lifestyles too distant from the culture of the poor, and politicization of the Church resulting from liberation theology), and to the vitality of the spiritual nature of Pentecostal denominations (which focus on direct relationships with God, opportunities for more personal involvement in the church, and firm moral discipline). Some of these explanations for Protestant growth were voiced earlier in the twentieth century but have been re-articulated in recent years with the advance of Pentecostalism.

As early as the 1940s Catholic prelates in Latin America warned against the invasion of Protestantism from the United States as a plot to destroy Catholicism. In 1942 Archbishop Sanabria of San José, Costa Rica, warned that: "Protestant proselytizing propaganda is an instrument of subjugation and imperialism. . . . If North American political protection is injurious to our Hispanic and Latin political traditions, religious protection is doubly harmful" (Bautz 1994, 7).

Since the 1970s these arguments have been reiterated both by the Vatican and by some Latin American Catholic bishops. In 1992 in an address to Latin American bishops meeting in Santo Domingo to celebrate the 500th anniversary of the discovery of the Americas, Pope John Paul II warned of "rapacious wolves" or "pseudo-spiritual movements" devouring Latin American Catholics, "causing division and discord in our communities," which are heavily funded from abroad (Cleary 1992c, 7).

In a widely quoted pastoral letter in January 1990 Archbishop Próspero Penados del Barrio of Guatemala denounced the "invasion of the sects" as an imperialist ploy by North Americans to promote their own political and business interests. He argued that the spread of Protestantism in Guatemala was, in fact, "more part of an economic and political strategy than a genuine religious interest" (Rose and Schultze 1993, 416). Some Mexican bishops voiced similar opinions in the early 1990s, claiming that the sects are a foreign threat to national security by creating discord and dividing communities in Mexico (Camp 1997, 95).

Sometimes Latin American bishops have even placed the blame on the CIA for subsidizing such denominations with money. The thrust of their argument is that the United States government wants to keep the poor of Latin America from remaining with the Catholic Church now that the bishops have become so critical of capitalism for failing to achieve equity for all (Stoll 1990, 33–34; McCoy 1989, 2; Camp 1997, 95).

A similar argument about foreign penetration has also been voiced by those who rely on Marxist analysis to explain international relations. In the late 1920s, Peruvian Marxist sociologist José Carlos Mariátegui criticized Protestantism in Latin America as an avenue of penetration for U.S. imperialism (Valcarcel 1972). In the mid-1980s this criticism was made again by some U.S. scholars and journalists. They argued that the U.S. government was subsidizing

Protestant missionaries in Central America to stop Marxist insurrection, as well as other popular movements critical of the United States, and was in the process destroying local indigenous culture (Westropp 1983; Huntington and Domínguez 1984; Merrill 1987; Assman 1987; Diamond 1989).

Since the 1960s other explanations have appeared which emphasize domestic factors in Latin America as being more responsible for the growth of Pentecostalism than foreign manipulation. These relate to the social upheaval stimulated by the breakup of the old hacienda system in the countryside and the subsequent migration of former peasants to large slums in cities. Two different streams of interpretation exist within this school, one concluding that Pentecostalism has produced harmful effects for society and the other pointing to positive consequences for the economy and politics.

In the late 1960s Swiss sociologist Christian Lalive d'Epinay, on the basis of research on Chilean, Brazilian, and Argentine Pentecostals, argued that such communities provided a haven for migrants who failed to find work in urban industry. Pentecostal churches served as countersocieties in shantytowns offering emotional support, strong personal relationships, and financial aid for uprooted persons. These churches, he argued, were also in continuity with the peasant culture they left in the countryside, since they duplicated the authoritarian nature of the hacienda—pastors maintained strict control over congregations, demanded total obedience of the faithful, and encouraged abstention from participation in secular organizations. Pentecostals, he claimed, are on "social strike" and live in "conformist disengagement" from a wider society that no longer offers them a meaningful identity (Lalive d'Epinay 1969, 128–45; 1975, 279).

Swiss historian Jean-Pierre Bastian, writing in the early 1990s, follows closely Lalive d'Epinay's argument. For him, Latin American Protestants associated with the mainline churches in the nineteenth and early twentieth centuries were middle-class reformers who built schools and businesses and participated in liberal political movements furthering democracy. The newer Pentecostal Protestants, he claims, are the marginalized and migratory poor. They seek refuge from a hostile world and combine their popular religious traditions of spiritism and veneration of saints with Pentecostal emotionalism and healing rituals. Bastian believes that these communities can serve as forms of resistance to modern social and economic models being imposed on the poor and are a means of protecting their ethnic and linguistic traditions. He sees Pentecostal communities, therefore, as much more active and creative in cultural defense than does Lalive d'Epinay, but he agrees that the internal workings of these communities are authoritarian and thus cannot act as social or political reform movements in the wider society (which they shun). He argues that they have assimilated the religious and political culture of repression associated with traditional Catholic and corporatist Latin America and, in turn, have come to support, tacitly and sometimes openly, political authoritarianism in society (Bastian 1990; 1992, 328–35, 342–45; 1993, 46–51).

German sociologist Émilio Willems did not believe Pentecostalism was producing cadres of psychologically maimed individuals seeking shelter from the cruel world and afraid of active citizenship. His study of Chilean and Brazilian Pentecostals in the early 1960s convinced him that the Protestant virtues of discipline, thrift, honesty, and sobriety were prevalent in these denominations and helped members take advantage of new economic opportunities opening up amidst the structural changes in society. Although poor, many experienced, he claimed, improvements in their lifestyles due to the elimination of alcohol from their lives, their new willingness to work hard and save, and their greater respect for women and the family unit as a whole. Willems was convinced that these experiences encouraged Pentecostals to aspire to middle-class status and eventually they would become active supporters of social reform. Although not yet an active political force in the early 1960s, he believed they were implicitly "genuine protagonists of democracy" since their new culture was a "symbolic subversion of the traditional social order" that had oppressed them (Willems 1967, 122–31, 166–67, 198, 228, 249).

British sociologist David Martin, building on Willems's work a generation later, believes these new denominations in fact are now having a positive transformative effect on society. Like Methodism in England, and later Pentecostalism in the United States, he views Pentecostalism in Latin America as a dynamic form of Protestantism opening up new cultural and social space for marginalized groups as they experience the hardships and uprootedness of the industrial revolution. These new churches provide their members with networks of support for adaptation and survival in new contexts.

Even if they have internal structures that are presently authoritarian, these communities are not just mirroring corporate cultural patterns of the past but are renewing a sense of self-esteem in individuals, providing them with moral discipline, communication skills, and ladders for leadership inside the congregation. These capacities may take two or three generations to come to fruition in wider society, but, as in England and the United States, he feels they will strengthen Latin American democracy in the long run by breaking the monopolistic Catholic control of culture and by inculcating values of equality, fraternity, and peaceability (D. Martin 1990, 22–25, 230–32, 264–68, 287–95).[2]

There are also arguments that focus on the failures of Catholicism in explaining the high conversion rates to Pentecostalism. Pope John Paul II at the 1992 Santo Domingo meeting, in addition to blaming foreign manipulation, acknowledged that the "great masses of Catholics are without adequate religious attention" due to the shortage of priests in Latin America (sometimes only one for every 10,000 baptized Catholics or more). He also claimed it can happen that "the faithful do not find in their pastoral ministers the strong sense of God" and that when this happens the poor "go to the sects seeking a religious sense of life" (Hansen 1992, 1; Cleary 1992c, 8). Clearly, he believes that some priests have neglected the spiritual needs of laity in favor of social and political commitments stemming from liberation theology (a major concern of the present pope, which is addressed below).

American anthropologist David Stoll elaborates on the same argument based on his study of Pentecostalism in Guatemala, Nicaragua, and Ecuador in the 1980s. He believes that Catholic communities, using liberation theology techniques of community organization and political mobilization to achieve social justice, have frightened away many peasants in Central America, since these groups have often incurred the wrath of the military. Pentecostal churches, in shunning such commitments, have been safer havens for the poor and have also nourished their deep need for spiritual sustenance amidst economic hardship and civil war (Stoll 1990, 39, 310–14; see also Lagos and Chacón 1987).

Others have pointed to the hunger for a more personal spirituality not found in Catholicism that provides meaning in a fragmented world (González Dorado 1992; Poblete and Galilea 1984). Some have underscored the centralized authority system, clericalism, and heavily rational theology still present in the Church which makes its bishops and priests distant from the popular culture of the poor (Comblin 1994, 206–7; C. Smith 1995, 8–9; Palma and Villela 1990, 27).

Finally, there are those scholars—Protestant and Catholic alike— who have underscored the vitality of Pentecostal spirituality and community life that they believe has been the major drawing factor in its rapid growth in contemporary Latin America. They argue that Pentecostalism meets the spiritual needs of the poor better than Catholicism due to its stress on direct personal encounters with God through prayers and simple explanation of the Scriptures by pastors (Wilson 1994, 101–3; Idígoras 1991, 242; Sepúlveda 1994, 72–77; Nuñez and Taylor 1989).

There are, therefore, a great variety of explanations as to why Pentecostalism is growing so rapidly in Latin America. Some could be considered complementary to one another—the aloofness of Catholicism and the spiritual vitality of Pentecostalism, social uprootedness of the poor and the community support offered by these new denominations. Other explanations, however, are diametrically opposed to one another and mutually exclusive—foreign intervention vs. genuine indigenous movements, communities nourishing individuality and equality vs. havens of escape with authoritarian overtones. Depending upon which explanations, or combinations thereof, are valid, the impact on society in the long run will be quite different—stimuli for economic growth, support for democratic values, "Trojan horses" for foreign interests, havens of escape undermining active citizenship, legitimacy for authoritarian regimes.

Before assessing the comparative validity of the various explanatory theories and their implications for society, it would be important to consider the changes occurring in Latin American Catholicism since the early 1980s. Catholicism is still the dominant religious force in the region and has been undergoing some significant changes since John Paul II became pope in 1978. Some are independent of Pentecostal growth, but others are directly aimed at making the Church more competitive and thus stopping the loss of baptized Catholics to Pentecostalism. The outcome of these new emphases in the Catholic Church can also have significant implications for social and political currents in wider society, especially to the extent that these changes in the Church interact with developments in Pentecostalism.

Ferment in Latin American Catholicism of the 1960s and 1970s

During the 1960s and 1970s most national Catholic churches in Latin America (with the notable exceptions of Argentina, Cuba, and Colombia) underwent significant internal transformations. In response to the call for reform in the universal Church authorized by the Second Vatican Council (1962–1965), Latin American bishops endorsed a decentralization of church structures into ecclesial base communities (*comunidades eclesiales de base*—CEBs) to give more responsibility to laity. They also urged a greater focus of pastoral efforts among the poor by priests and nuns and proclaimed a commitment by the institutional Church to protect the dignity and human rights of all (CELAM II 1970). Their particular concern was to place the Church in a better competitive position with Marxists and thus prevent the loss of working-class Catholics to leftist political parties or revolutionary movements which were on the rise in the late 1960s and early 1970s in several countries of the region.

Latin American Catholic theologians, many writing from a context of new social and pastoral involvement with the life of the poor in Peru, Brazil, Chile, El Salvador, and Nicaragua, began to articulate a new vision for the Church in the late 1960s and 1970s. They espoused various types of liberation theology, all of which called for a Church that combines preaching the gospel and administering the sacraments with a deep commitment to social justice. The Scriptures were to be read from the perspective of the poor and sin was to be understood not only in personal but also institutional terms. Unjust economic and social structures were as sinful as personally failing to observe one of the Ten Commandments since they cause pain to the poor. The Church, they argued, must announce in word and action an integral form of salvation, or liberation, from all manifestations of sin, and not merely offer individuals the means of personal salvation through the sacraments. The Church must struggle against every form of repression in society and support officially leftist political movements and parties (even those that use violence as a last resort) if these aim at bringing about democratic socialism, the only political and economic system compatible with the Gospel (Gutiérrez 1973; Segundo 1973; Miranda 1974; Assman 1976; Dussel 1976; Boff 1978).[3]

These pastoral and theological changes did enable the Church to play a significant role in societal reforms underway in Latin America in the 1960s and early 1970s. Bishops in several nations supported agrarian and tax changes, expanded suffrage, and increased government spending in health, education, and popular housing. With financial assistance from Catholic organizations in Europe, Canada, and the United States, local clergy started social programs which promoted literacy training, buying and selling cooperatives, and peasant unions among the rural poor. Priests and nuns also created revolving credit funds, low-income housing construction, and basic health projects in burgeoning urban slums. Local base communities (CEBs) were formed in both rural and urban areas which included Bible study, training for lay preachers and catechists, and prayer groups. All of these new social and religious commitments revitalized the Church at the local level in low-income areas and also helped to further the reform process in society (B. Smith 1982, 1990; Bruneau 1974, 1982; Levine 1981, 1992).

In the mid- and late-1970s, when almost all Latin American countries (except Colombia and Venezuela) experienced military rule, these new programs and base communities of the Church expanded in scope and number. They provided material and legal assistance to those persecuted for political reasons, as well as logistical support for these fleeing persecution and trying to avail themselves of the right of political asylum in foreign embassies. Catholic bishops also became one of the few sources of public criticism against these abuses, as many prelates individually and collectively denounced torture, summary executions, forced disappearances, and suspension of due process of law. Church leaders were also active supporters of an early withdrawal of the military from power in several countries (B. Smith 1979, 1982; Berryman 1984; Levine 1992; Bruneau 1982; Dussel 1992).

All of these new social and political commitments made the Catholic Church a more credible ally of the poor, peaceful reform, and constitutional government than it had ever been before in Latin

America. There were, however, considerable costs incurred by the Church for such commitments.

Priests formed organizations to support socialist movements, and a few joined guerrilla or Marxist movements (in Argentina, Chile, Colombia, Peru, Nicaragua). They often clashed openly with their bishops over the extent to which official representatives of the Church should become involved in partisan politics and over the role of local church communities in ecclesiastical decision-making (Dodson 1979, 1986; B. Smith 1982; Dodson and O'Shaugnessy 1990). Upper-income Catholics verbally attacked the hierarchy for their public criticisms of military governments, and in some countries (Argentina, Brazil, Chile) they formed protest organizations demanding a return to a more spiritually focused Catholicism and one that required obedience to government. Secret police and right-wing terrorist organizations harassed priests, nuns, and lay leaders active in human rights campaigns or social service projects among the poor in Central America and the Southern Cone region throughout the 1970s. In some cases this led to the exile, forced or voluntary, of clergy and religious, and in other instances precipitated their imprisonment, torture, or murder. In some national Catholic churches, already thin in local leadership and relying for one-half or more of their personnel on foreign priests and nuns, such confrontations left Catholicism even more understaffed (Lernoux 1980, 1989).

Vatican Attempts at Church Retrenchment and Their Implications

Just at the time when Pentecostalism began to grow significantly in Latin America, Catholicism underwent some serious crises. As mentioned earlier, Pope John Paul II expressed strong concern that local Catholic leaders betrayed some of their primary pastoral responsibilities. From the beginning of his term in October 1978, Pope John Paul II has taken steps to pull many national Catholic churches in Latin America back from what he considers their overinvolvement in social and political issues. He has affirmed the Church's support for social justice, human rights, and democracy, but asserts that the primary focus of priests, nuns, and lay leaders must be on the celebration of the sacraments and on the spiritual formation of the laity. He has forbidden involvement in partisan political movements by those officially representing the Church (priests, religious, lay deacons, and CEB leaders) and has suspended clergy who take positions in governments, notably in Nicaragua in the 1980s (Dodson and O'Shaugnessy 1990).

Pope John Paul II has consistently replaced retiring bishops (many of them progressives appointed by Popes John XXIII or Paul VI) with priests who have not been known for their strong social commitments but who have been publicly supportive of official Church positions on birth control, abortion, and maintaining a male celibate priesthood. In Brazil, one of the most progressive national Catholic churches, between 1978 and 1990 he named 128 new bishops (in a hierarchy of 274 at that time period), and of these at least 97 were known to be theological conservatives (Martins 1990).

Under this pope the Vatican Curia has been more vigilant about Latin American theological developments and seminary training. The Sacred Congregation on Doctrine of the Faith has issued statements critical of some positions espoused by liberation theologians. One prominent figure, Leonardo Boff in Brazil, was silenced more than once before resigning from the priesthood in frustration. Some liberal seminaries have been closed after critical evaluations by official visitors from the Vatican, while the faculty and curricula of others have been reoriented to emphasize prayer, biblical scholarship, Church history, canon law, and personal spiritual counseling (Stewart-Gambino 1994, 131; Serbin 1992, 404–5; Fleet and B. Smith 1997, 5).

All of these efforts by Rome have strengthened the position of conservative Latin American prelates. Some bishops have moved liberation-oriented priests out of socially involved poor parishes. In some countries they have sent foreign missionaries known for their theologically and pastorally progressive stances back home (or not defended them when critical public officials have lifted their residency visas). Other bishops have insisted on strict public loyalty from the nuns and priests in their dioceses to official Church teachings on sexual morality and have also demanded a more spiritual focus in local church ministries.

These strategies by the pope, the Roman Curia, and some theologically conservative bishops, have attempted to prevent local base
community leaders in Latin America, in their eagerness to alleviate the suffering of the poor, from neglecting the traditional hall-
marks of Roman Catholicism—obedience to hierarchical authority,
celebration of the sacraments as the central means of receiving
God's saving grace, and concern for the spiritual welfare of all regardless of class. An added objective behind these attempts to pull
the Latin American Church back from intense social and political
involvements (especially at the grassroots level) has been to make it
more competitive with Pentecostalism that stresses primarily spiritual objectives.

The success of these efforts to reorient the Church in a more
traditional direction, and whether there will be adjustments in their
implementation, will affect both the moral and religious priorities
inside the Latin American Catholic Church and its impact in society
at large. As in the case of Pentecostalism, various interpretations
have been offered as to where the Church is headed.

Should the retrenchment be successful, Church leaders and activists might very well become occupied primarily with a spiritual
agenda and the internal affairs of the institution and only address
developments in society insofar as these directly affect the Church.
Local base communities would continue to be training grounds for
laity, but social projects would be de-emphasized in favor of spiritual
activities such as prayer, Bible study, preparation for the sacraments,
and individual pastoral counseling. Members of these groups would
not be encouraged to involve themselves in politics except to defend
official Catholic teachings and interests. This, in effect, would be
a return to the posture of the pre–Vatican II and pre–Medellín
Catholicism that was tacitly, and sometimes explicitly, identified
with Latin American socioeconomic elites and conservative political
movements favorable to the Church.[4]

However, it may be that such efforts by the Vatican to reorient
the Latin American Church will not be successful, or only will be
so among the new bishops it is hand-picking. These conservative
prelates may attempt to pull the Church back but local-level priests,
nuns, and lay leaders committed to social justice and the economic needs of the poor may resist such directives. This could

stimulate serious tensions between higher and lower leaders, or out-
right schism in the Church depending on how severe the differences
become and what strategies each side decides to pursue. This could
split Catholicism into two churches in Latin America—a smaller
spiritual-oriented Catholicism constituted primarily of the upper
and middle classes (currently no more than 20 percent of the population), and a larger popular Church, unconcerned about maintaining ties with the bishops or serving all classes but deeply involved
in the struggles of workers and peasants seeking to redress social
and political grievances.[5]

A third possibility is that this is a period of internal adjustment
in which the Vatican is slowing the process of change underway in
Latin American Catholicism so that it can be better integrated into
the Church's traditional religious mission. The hierarchy is emphasizing internal discipline and spiritual formation of clergy and laity
so as to keep these vital as new social commitments are undertaken.
Spiritual activities and Church discipline are not meant to replace a
concern for social equity, human rights, and democratic values in
politics but are being re-emphasized after a period of intense local
church activism so that a balance might be restored among the various dimensions.

This scenario assumes that there still is an overall consensus in
favor of Church support for social reform at the hierarchical and
local levels of the institution. It downplays the plausibility of either
a reactionary or a chronically polarized (and possibly schismatic)
Church emerging in the future in favor of one in which higher and
lower leaders collaborate in spiritual and social commitments. Local
base communities in this scenario will continue to act as training
grounds for citizens actively engaged in societal reform and democratic politics in their respective societies, but they will also become
more devout and loyal Catholics in the process.[6]

These scenarios are quite different both in their implications
for the future direction of the Catholic Church but also for Latin
American society as a whole. Despite the rapid growth of Pentecostalism, Catholicism still remains the religion of the vast majority
in Latin America. How it digests official efforts of the Vatican at
retrenchment can have a significant impact on the stability of recently constituted democracies after a decade or more of military
rule in many Latin American nations.

Possible Pentecostal/Catholic Scenarios in the Future

Although there has been considerable research on the changing composition of Protestantism, and some on the new directions of Catholicism, none has looked comparatively at trends going on in both denominations, the interrelationships between them, and the combined societal impact their religious dynamics are likely to have in the years ahead. Both branches are now considerably rooted in working-class culture and their credibility among the poor far outweighs that of most political parties. Their active participants taken together far outnumber the total number of citizens involved in all other kinds of voluntary associations combined—cultural, political, recreational (Berryman 1994b). In fact, some scholars have argued that Catholic base communities and Pentecostal churches are the most powerful forces in the creation of community life at the grassroots level in Latin America today (Froehle 1995, 27). Pentecostalism and Catholicism directly affect millions of religiously committed Latin Americans, and, through their choices and involvements, millions more indirectly.

In examining synthetically the various interpretations and scenarios articulated above about trends underway in each camp, it appears that several combined trajectories are possible. Some will be supportive of whatever political regime is in power, some will create some bitter internecine religious tensions that could complicate politics, some could be manipulated by clever political leaders interested in gaining or preserving a position in government, some might be supportive, tacitly or openly, of authoritarian movements, and some could promote expanding equity within a democratic framework. The remaining part of this section will sketch the various scenarios that could emerge from the interactions of Pentecostalism and Catholicism in Latin America in the next decade.

(1) Mutual Flight from the World. One possible outcome would be a tandem reinforcement by both denominations of a flight from secular involvements. If the assessments of Lalive d'Epinay and Bastian are correct for Pentecostalism, and the retrenchment going on within the Catholic Church brings it back to resemble traditional Catholicism, both denominations could reinforce one another in stressing primarily otherworldly goals for their respective

members. Pentecostal and Catholic local congregations would, in fact, come to resemble each other. Each would emphasize primarily the spiritual formation of laity and downplay the importance of belonging to social or political organizations; and each would emphasize personal relationship with Jesus Christ, obedience to church authority, and evangelizing new members as the prime Christian responsibilities.

This scenario would, however, have some significant political implications, despite its otherworldly emphasis. If both traditions emphasized primarily spiritual concerns together they could have a powerful dampening effect on citizenship. Their respective local communities could draw off many potential leaders and activists for community organizations and political parties. Electoral participation might even decline among members of both churches.

Moreover, if the "refuge from the world" scenario becomes the dominant pattern for both Catholicism and Pentecostalism there will be a decline of public moral statements by church leaders on critical societal issues. If the new majority in Protestantism and the vast number of Catholics turn their primary attention to otherworldly concerns, clerics and lay leaders in the next generation may be much less willing to exercise a prophetic voice on behalf of the poor and against abuses of power. They may refrain from denouncing injustice and violations of human rights and no longer give their moral support for democratic processes and values in society—a valiant role played by many pastors from historic Protestant churches and Catholic clergy from the 1960s to the 1980s. Thus, the moral framework necessary for a stable democracy could lose some important reinforcement in the public forum.

(2) Conflicting Religiopolitical Agendas. It is also possible that Pentecostalism and Catholicism in the years ahead will move in very different directions from one another. It could happen, for example, that Pentecostalism fulfills the expectations of those scholars (Willems 1967; D. Martin 1990; C. Smith 1995; Dodson 1997) who see it as a strong modernizing force for capitalist development and liberal democracy, while Catholicism returns to a primarily spiritual force with affinities for political authoritarianism and state controls on markets.[7]

Currently, there is an economic restructuring underway in most

Latin American nations removing controls on private exchange, dismantling public enterprises, reducing public services, drastically lowering tariff barriers, and offering substantial tax and labor incentives to foreign investors—all within the political framework of recently reconstituted democracies. If Pentecostalism serves as a stimulant of a strong work ethic and encourages freedom, individuality, and responsibility, then it could give an important boost to the current economic and political strategies now in vogue in Latin America. If these models succeed in meeting the needs of the majority better than strategies of state capitalism which prevailed over the past half-century in Latin America, the public moral voice of Catholicism might become less relevant since its traditional preference for state intervention in the economy would appear outmoded under such circumstances.

On the other hand, the above roles could be reversed. Catholicism may be merely undergoing a period of adjustment in order to accommodate in more orderly fashion modern values of freedom, equity, and democracy. If so, its clergy will continue to play a strong public role in word and action in favor of social justice, human rights, and constitutionalism and its cadres of laity trained in base communities will act as a leaven in politics favorable to moderate reform movements. Pentecostalism may not turn out to be the modernizing force its spiritual cousins have been in England and the United States, but rather serve as a haven for those too broken ever to better themselves economically and to participate as conscientious citizens. Its internal mechanisms for tight clerical control of laity might also inculcate values antithetical to political democracy and more attune to authoritarianism.

Moreover, if Catholicism and Protestantism take opposing moral positions (or one is silent and the other vocal) on such critical public issues as citizen participation in politics, community service to promote the common good, nonviolent strategies to achieve social change, the sacrosanct nature of private property, equity for the poor, the inviolability of fundamental human rights, and the desirability of representative government, divisive religiopolitical battles could ensue. Socioeconomic groups could appeal to different denominations to justify morally those policies serving their own special interests rather than the common good. Political movements favoring and those opposing authoritarian solutions to societal

problems could each justify their respective positions by appealing to different Christian churches. Radical political movements
impatient with the pace of change in newly constituted democracies
might make alliances with liberation theology Christians so as to
gain moral legitimacy for aggressive forms of protest. All of these
developments would involve political manipulation of Christianity,
and this would seriously limit its capacity for articulating the moral
underpinnings of a stable and just democracy in Latin America.

(3) Prophetic Social Catalysts. A final possibility for Pentecostalism
and Catholicism in Latin America would be a gradual convergence
of both in support of styles of citizenship and public policy that
favor economic development, social equity, and constitutionalism.
Both traditions in Latin America now share some common characteristics—decentralized structures, formation of deeply committed,
rather than merely nominal, lay Christians, and the enhancement of
self-esteem and a sober life-style among members (Mariz 1994b).
Moreover, they are now the two most vital cultural movements
among the poor in most Latin American countries. What may happen is that these commonly shared values, styles, and objectives will
bring the two denominations closer together in the years ahead not
only religiously but also in collaborative social ventures.

Even if Pentecostal pastors and Catholic bishops want to avoid
entangling political involvements, prolonged personal exposure to
popular culture and an emerging articulate laity rooted in the working classes may force them to take public critical moral stances on
social and economic issues. The dislocations associated with trans-
forming economies into unrestricted market systems, that have been
for more than half a century under considerable state controls, are
creating severe hardships for the poor. Conservative Pentecostal pastors and Catholic bishops alike may have to exercise a prophetic
voice to remind policymakers of such high social costs if they are
to maintain credibility among their respective congregations suffering the brunt of the policies. A collaborative prophetic stance by
Pentecostal and Catholic clergy could force limits on the pace and
style of economic change underway, preventing further aggravation
of economic differences and guaranteeing a more stable social basis
for newly reconstituted democracies.[8]

It may be that common concerns about the poor will bring clergy from both traditions to a shared understanding of their mission. Ecumenical cooperation could emerge in the decades ahead which would promote exchange of information on effective pastoral strategies in popular areas. Interdenominational dialogue could also produce common prophetic statements on public policy issues affecting both Pentecostals and Catholics. Interchurch structures could develop, leading to the pooling of financial resources to support cooperatively sponsored social services for peasants and workers.

Some believe that significant cultural transformations are underway throughout Latin America due to religion, and that these could significantly alter the contours of society (Levine 1992, 1996). The poor have constituted between 70 and 80 percent of every Latin American country since colonial times. Many have been locked into a culture of passivity so that they are objects of the choices of others rather than active agents of their own fate. If Pentecostal congregations and Catholic base communities alike train increasing numbers of working-class laity who have come to an appreciation of their own self-worth, have begun to better themselves economically, and in the process learned communication and leadership skills, such persons might then for the first time take active roles as citizens and demand that society take their views seriously. If so, their sheer numbers could make the difference in creating a sound basis for democratic reform politics for years to come.

The next two chapters of this book will examine recent developments in Latin American Pentecostalism and Catholicism respectively. The purpose is to provide a basis on which to judge the validity of the various theories about the nature and implications of the changes underway in both traditions. In the concluding chapter, I shall return to the three future scenarios laid out above in order to assess their relative plausibility given the dominant religious and social tendencies current in both denominations.

2

EXPLANATIONS AND IMPLICATIONS OF PENTECOSTAL GROWTH

The various explanations in the literature cited earlier about the reasons for, and implications of, Pentecostal growth can be clustered into three different categories: (1) an invasion from abroad orchestrated by U.S. Protestantism and the U.S. government, (2) a creative response to socioeconomic upheavals within Latin America that offers significant economic and social benefits to its new adherents, (3) an authoritarian haven for social misfits that breeds attitudes of dependency and gives open or tacit support to right-wing political movements. The current evidence for each of these theories will be considered below in sequence.

1. Invasion from Abroad

There is a long history of U.S. missionary activity in Latin America, dating back to the latter part of the nineteenth century. This early history, however, was dominated by mainline Protestant churches. U.S. Evangelical missionary efforts (including Assemblies of God, the Central American Mission, Seventh-Day Adventists, Wycliffe Bible Translators, and various independent "faith missions") did not begin in earnest until the 1920s and 1930s. These intensified after World War II and by the 1960s surpassed the number of missionaries from Lutheran, Presbyterian, Episcopalian, Methodist, and Baptist churches. Evangelical denominations did maintain close ties to sending churches in the United States, and used U.S. money to build a series of schools, hospitals, Bible study institutes, and radio stations throughout Latin America (Huntington and Domínguez 1984, 3–10; Greenway 1994, 187–91; Goffin 1994, 35–76). By the 1970s and 1980s these efforts were supplemented by various parachurch agencies associated with Evangelical denominations in the United States, such as Campus Crusade for Christ, World Vision International, and the Christian Broadcast Network. These groups brought printed materials, food, clothing, medicines, and radio and television programs featuring (in translation) U.S. religious evangelists (Deiros 1991, 150–51; Greenway 1994, 91–95; Huntington and Domínguez 1984, 18–19; Rose and Schultze 1993, 434; Goffin 1994, 77–90).

Beginning in the 1950s, the U.S. government began to establish close ties to American missionaries in Latin American countries (Colby and Dennett 1995). During the Cold War the Central Intelligence Agency (CIA) used missionaries in Chile, Ecuador, Bolivia, and Brazil as sources of information about grassroots movements that might be sympathetic to Marxism. The United States Agency for International Development (USAID) also channeled U.S. foreign aid to church-sponsored socioeconomic projects in several Latin American countries during these years as bulwarks to stop communism (Lernoux 1989, 281–310).

Although U.S. Senate hearings on CIA activities in 1975 resulted in restrictions on CIA involvement with church personnel abroad, these were loosened by President Reagan in 1981 (Stoll 1990, 148). In the mid-1980s, amidst U.S. government efforts to block Marxism in Central America, Evangelical church groups in the United States raised private money (with the encouragement of the White House) to further U.S. interests in that region. Evangelical groups channeled relief supplies to the Contras who were fighting the Sandinistas in Nicaragua and also brought in church money to Guatemala to assist in the government-sponsored resettlement of indigenous peoples into "strategic hamlets" where they would be out of the reach of both Marxist guerrillas and Catholic priests and nuns. Televangelist Pat Robertson and his Christian Broadcast Network were very visible in this aid project ("Operation Lovelift") along with business associations linked with U.S. Evangelical churches (Brouwer, Gifford, and Rose 1996, 56).

In addition to raising money Evangelicals also carried on a public relations and lobby campaign in the United States in favor of governments which the U.S. government supported in Central America (most notably Guatemala and El Salvador) and against others (Sandinista-controlled Nicaragua). Moreover, mysterious "salary supplements" were distributed to conservative Protestant pastors in

Nicaragua from North American Christians with close associations with the U.S. government. The literature and preaching of American Evangelical groups such as Campus Crusade for Christ in both El Salvador and Nicaragua during the 1980s were heavily laced with anti-communist rhetoric with an implicit message that the United States represented true Christianity (Stoll 1990, 250–53; Deiros 1991, 177–78; Lernoux 1989, 157–62; Huntington and Domínguez 1984, 30–33; Peck 1984, 184–88).

A strong case can be made that some Pentecostal pastors in Central America during the Reagan years willingly became channels of U.S. religious and government money that was given to them for a political purpose. It is also clear that U.S. Evangelical groups both in the United States and in Central America had high visibility as supporters of U.S. interests in Central America during the 1980s. There are, therefore, grounds for the "invasion" theory. Some scholars who have studied this evidence closely, in fact, have underscored the damage done to the credibility of Pentecostalism because of willing collaboration with U.S. political interests in parts of Latin America in the 1980s (Stoll 1990, xv, 321–28; Goffin 1994, 95–98).

However, even more cogent evidence exists that Catholicism is dependent on foreign support and at times has also collaborated with foreign government interests. The Catholic Church has been in Latin America far longer than Pentecostal Protestantism and is even more dependent on foreign personnel and financial support. More than one-half of the Catholic priests in most Latin American countries are foreign-born since the requirements for the priesthood (celibacy and considerable education) have made it unappealing or placed it out of reach of the vast majority of Latin American males. Moreover, the financial support for Catholic religious and social projects among the poor in Latin America are almost entirely financed by Catholic churches or social agencies from Europe, Canada, and the United States. The largest international Catholic charitable agencies that assist Church programs in Latin America also receive considerable amounts of their money from the governments in their home countries (B. Smith 1979, 1982).

Catholic Relief Services (CRS) in the United States, for example, has long depended on USAID subsidies in food, cash grants, and freight cost reimbursements for over two-thirds of its resources each year. In addition, U.S. government aid often comes with restrictions. During the Cold War it could not be used in any country with a Marxist government (Cuba or Sandinista Nicaragua), and sometimes was tailored to promote U.S. anti-drug objectives in certain countries of Latin America (B. Smith 1990, 113–16, 171–75, 294, 299–306). Moreover, in the midst of the Reagan years (1983–84) USAID gave considerably more assistance to CRS for its overseas activities ($264 million) than to eight of the largest U.S. Evangelical aid agencies ($31 million) (Stoll 1990, 271–72).

Furthermore, when the evidence came to light that the CIA routinely was using U.S. missionaries in Latin America as sources for information in the 1950s and 1960s and channeling money to them for their social programs, it was not merely those with ties to Evangelical Christianity who were involved. Catholic clergy were cultivated as informants and some Catholic organizations received financial support (Lernoux 1989, 281–310). As late as 1987 it was reported that some of the programs supported by Archbishop Miguel Obando y Bravo in Managua, a staunch critic of the Sandinista regime, came indirectly from the CIA (Stoll 1990, 99).

It is clear, therefore, that the criticism of being heavily dependent on foreign sources of support and acting on behalf of foreign interests can be leveled at Roman Catholicism in Latin America, not just at Pentecostalism. Many of those who make the charge of "invasion" are, in fact, Latin American Catholic clergy and Vatican officials who overlook the vulnerability of their own Church to the same charges (Froehle 1997, 213–14).

More importantly, however, when one examines the contours of Pentecostalism itself in Latin America there are strong indicators that, despite foreign linkages explained above, it is a truly indigenous movement whose growth and sustenance do not depend primarily on foreign support. Leaders come from popular sectors and remain close to the poor since the training they receive is much less academic than that of Catholic priests, and largely consists of apprenticeship or "on-the-job" learning. They thus resonate with the mind and culture of those whom they serve and are far more charismatic preachers than most priests (Idígoras 1991, 245–46; Berg and Pretiz 1996a and 1996b; Cleary and Sepúlveda 1997, 108–9; Froehle 1997, 210.)

The vast majority of these churches have little financial aid from outside the country for their pastoral work (Wilson 1997, 145).

Pastors' salaries are supplied in large part by the requirement of tithing by members (payment of up to one-tenth of one's income to the church). Pentecostal churches function at the grassroots level in poor areas. In some countries they now have national networks linking their churches, but they do not carry on extensive social projects for the wider community as do many local Catholic base communities. Their focus is on spiritual activities that require little financial outlay (D. Martin 1990, 195–98; Mariz 1994a, 82–87; Froehle 1997, 213).

The larger social institutions maintained by Pentecostals—schools, hospitals, charitable projects, radio and television programs, massive open air rallies in stadiums—do require financial support from Evangelical churches and agencies from abroad (Brouwer, Gifford, and Rose 1996, 61–62, 68–73). The written materials available for those who are literate still are, by and large, translations of American and European authors. Some of these larger structural commitments, however, are becoming more indigenous in financing and character. Many of the schools that the Assemblies of God now run are attracting members of the middle and upper-middle classes and are beginning to rely on parent tuition. Many of the media programs are now produced in Latin America, not in the United States, and are attuned to local culture and spiritual tastes (Rose and Schultze 1993, 431, 434; Gutwirth 1991, 102, 110, 111).

The Universal Church of the Kingdom of God in Brazil, founded in 1977 by Pentecostal pastor Edir Macedo with a membership of 3.5 million by the mid-1990s, generates over $700 million annually in donations from laity and earnings from its enterprises. The Church owns the third largest television network in Brazil, operates thirty radio stations, and publishes a weekly newspaper with a circulation of 700,000. It has also created satellite churches in thirty-five other countries, including the United States, Europe, and Africa (Serbin 1997, 8; Shaull 1996). This is a remarkable case of institution-building and financial autonomy. There are some others that enjoy material blessings as well who employ an urban "megachurch" approach similar to that which characterizes successful Evangelical churches in the United States. These cases tend to be exceptions rather than the rule, however, and most Pentecostal congregations in Latin America are small and informal and lack the institutional trappings of these well-healed groups (Jeffrey 1996a, 7).

One major reason is that the institutional means of spreading the message and attracting converts are not nearly as successful as are personal contacts through door-to-door campaigns and family ties (Greenway 1994, 199; Marzal 1989, 392; Jeffrey 1996a, 7). Members of Pentecostal churches are required to act as missionaries spreading the faith and bringing in new members, and these proselytization efforts have nothing to do with foreign personnel or finances. In fact, what makes Pentecostalism most attractive are the face-to-face testimonies of friends, neighbors, and relatives and the witness of the personal, moral, and spiritual transformations that have occurred in their lives after conversion (Aubry 1990, 111; Idígoras 1991, 243–44; Cook 1985, 178–80; Galilea W. 1992, 8).

The conclusion of most scholars who have studied Latin American Pentecostalism closely is that it is a genuinely popular phenomenon driven by the missionary zeal of its local converts. Even if beholden to foreign missionaries for its origins and for some of its current institutions, and despite the support given by some of its pastors to U.S. government objectives (primarily in Central America in the 1980s), these are insufficient to explain its strong drawing power throughout Latin America, especially among the poor (Escobar 1994, 27–29; Damen 1987, 52–55; Berryman 1994a, 150–58, 1994b, 21–23; Westmeier 1993, 76; Hollenweger 1986; Deiros 1991, 179–81; Rose and Schultze 1993, 443; Levine 1996; Cleary and Sepúlveda 1997, 98–101).

Franz Damen, a Belgian Catholic missionary in Bolivia, concludes that Pentecostalism is not a "gigantic mass that in a sudden, violent, and uncontrollable way throws itself upon an innocent and unarmed population" from abroad. The truth, he claims, is that these denominations "rely rather on a relatively good reception on the part of the people" (Damen 1987, 47, 55).

There is much evidence that the primary benefits offered by Pentecostalism are not promises sustained by foreign powers but rather a vision for a better life and the moral resources necessary to persevere in it (Aubry 1990, 112; Westmeier 1993, 76; Berryman 1994b, 25).

2. Means of Economic Advancement

Some believe that the growth of Pentecostalism in Latin America is a result of the dislocations caused by economic modernization.

They argue that it equips its new adherents with skills and attitudes to take advantage of new opportunities that are created by these changes (Willems 1967; D. Martin 1990; Marcom 1990; Tapia 1995). It sometimes occurs that Pentecostal pastors themselves make the claim that new members improve their economic status after conversion (Flora 1976; Hoffnagel 1978; Novaes 1985). Some of these assessments are also based on assumptions that the type of modern economic development that has occurred in countries with a predominantly Protestant cultural heritage (most notably England and the United States) might be replicated in Latin America now that Protestantism is breaking the cultural religious monopoly of Catholicism (D. Martin 1990; Novak 1982).

A close examination of the empirical studies that have been conducted on the relationship of conversions to Pentecostalism and economic advancement are not conclusive. Studies indicate that some structural transformations in the economy are associated with conversions—changes in land-holding patterns in the countryside, migration to cities, and the decline of job opportunities in industry. Many indicate that there is also an improvement in the life-style of people negatively affected by such changes once they join Pentecostal churches. However, no consensus exists as to the significance of economic improvement that occurs, nor are there solid indications that continued advancement will be possible beyond a minimal first gain.

Some studies have shown that tightly-knit Pentecostal communities can be a means of resisting loss of indigenous culture and a protection against incursions by new large land-holding classes against traditional small farmers or indigenous peoples (Bastian 1985; Garma Navarro 1987; Kanagy 1995). They can also be a source of assistance after a natural disaster or a war has caused serious economic losses in a region (Garrard-Burnett 1986). It is also clear, however, that those who are able to experience upward social mobility are those who already have some stable wealth and are thus able to move into new economic arrangements (from land-holding to small-scale artisanry or petty commerce). It is also true that foreign sources of aid from Evangelical churches in the United States are the critical means to give such persons a boost (Bastian 1985; Kanagy 1995; Garrard-Burnett 1986). Moreover, the pastors in Pentecostal churches are the ones who most significantly improve their incomes due to the requirement that congregations make tithing contributions to support them (Mariz 1994a, 86).

In some countries, such as Guatemala, there is an expanding presence of Pentecostal churches among the middle and upper-middle classes who already are financially established. Rather than offering these groups the means for economic advancement, the "prosperity theology" that Pentecostals preach to better-off converts legitimizes their relatively comfortable status as a reward for true faith and hard work (Brouwer, Gifford, and Rose 1996, 59, 52–67). These converts, termed "neo-Pentecostals" by some scholars, are clearly in the minority. They also seem to have the highest degree of recidivism since their commitments to their new denominations are less permanent than those of poor converts (Hallum 1996, 50, 62, 106–7).

The more common pattern that emerges in the literature is that there is some tangible, albeit minimal, improvement in the economic condition for low-income converts, not because of new economic opportunities they are better able to exploit nor material aid from outside, but from their own changed personal consumption patterns. Pentecostals no longer have to pay what some have called a "cultural tax" that poor Catholics are expected to contribute to their local communities—support for local religious fiestas and the alcohol consumption that often accompanies these celebrations. In addition, Pentecostal churches make a greater effort than Catholic base communities in getting husbands to accompany their wives to church and to give up drinking, gambling, smoking, and frequenting prostitutes that are part of machismo culture in Latin America. The conjugal unit is thus strengthened and the prosperity of the family increases due to more cash on hand (sometimes from 20 percent to 40 percent more) that otherwise would have been spent by the husband on his personal pleasures (Annis 1987, 140–42; 1985; Rolim 1985; Mariz 1994a, 129–30; Brusco 1993, 147; 1995, 144–46).

A Pentecostal community also offers understanding to the poor in an emotionally supportive community that will listen to their pain, treat them with seriousness, and do what little it can to help them cope (Froehle 1997, 212). By strengthening the family unit itself by attacking some of the patterns of behavior associated with machismo, it uplifts the dignity of women and children and significantly reduces tensions and abuses stemming from the male neglect of responsibilities. Personal family relationships improve, memberships in a warm, loving community result, and modest improvements are made in diet and clothing for parents and children—all very important improvements in the quality of life for the poor. (Roberts 1968; Flora 1976; Goldin and Metz 1991; Mariz 1994a, 40–42; Drogus 1997, 62–64; Williams 1997, 187).

In most instances, these improvements do not, however, lead to a significant advance in social mobility or employment for Pentecostals. Literacy training is not common in Pentecostal churches, except up to the point that one can read some of the Bible. Job training or placement is not a major undertaking, although fellow church members are conscientious in helping one another search out existing employment opportunities and in giving hospitality to Pentecostal migrants newly arrived in cities until they find shelter of their own. Pentecostal churches will also use some of their tithes to pay the burial expenses of destitute members and buy food for their unemployed members. For most converts, Pentecostalism thus helps its members survive poverty better than they otherwise would and to prevent their condition from worsening further. However, it does not offer the means to advance significantly beyond one's economic level (Roberts 1968; Mariz 1994a 40–42, 84–87; Flora 1976; Mariz 1994a 40–42, 84–87; Bowen 1996, 121–23; Froehle 1997, 216).

Pentecostal communities do emphasize attitudes necessary for economic advancement. Commitment to a frugal life-style, saving one's earnings, and limiting one's consumption to necessities are all part of the ethic stressed by pastors. Some studies have shown, however, that these attitudes and behavior do not just appear for the first time after conversion to Pentecostalism but are part of the essential ingredients for countless numbers of poor in Latin America whether they are Pentecostal or not.

Cecilia Mariz in her study of Pentecostal congregations and Catholic base communities (CEBs) in Recife and Rio de Janeiro, Brazil, found little difference between Pentecostals and Catholic CEB members in commitment to a work ethic, to savings, and to avoiding unnecessary consumption (Mariz 1994a, 121–30). Liliana Goldin and Brent Metz in their study of highland Guatemalan Mayas also found what they called "invisible converts" to the Protestant work ethic among sizable numbers of poor Catholics in the same region who had also suffered dislocations due to land loss. In attempting to survive, they displayed many of the same moral codes as did Pentecostals: hard work, frugality, commitment to the family unit, valuing of competition in the workplace, and restructured leisure activities to cut down on spending (Goldin and Metz 1991, 335–36).

A factor complicating the chances of the poor—Pentecostal or Catholic—from using these attitudes and minimal safety nets as a launching pad to escape poverty has been the restructuring of the economy that has been going on throughout Latin America during the 1980s and early 1990s. In order to pay back mounting foreign debts and to attract new capital from abroad, Latin American governments have been selling off state enterprises in industry, agriculture, and services to the private sector, reducing social spending in health and education, cutting back on subsidies and price controls in basic food and transportation, lowering tariff barriers to let in more goods from abroad, and offering tax and labor incentives to foreign investors. Inflation has declined, new foreign loans and investments have been forthcoming, and overall growth rates have soared throughout the region. The poor, however, have experienced steady economic decline in the process.

Reports both from the World Bank (IBRD) and the United Nations Economic Commission for Latin America (ECLAC) have shown that the rate of increase in poverty in Latin America and the Caribbean jumped from 27 percent to 32 percent between 1980 and 1989. Unemployment now exceeds 10 percent in most countries, and when the numbers of the underemployed (making below the minimum wage) are included the statistic may reach 50 percent or more. On average, 1990 incomes were about what they were in 1970 in real terms, with purchasing power dropping 40 percent during the 1980s. The overall number of people living below the poverty line (earning $2 a day or less in 1985 U.S. dollars) went from 170 million in 1986 to 183 million in 1989 to 266 million in 1990. It is expected to reach 296 million (or about 64 percent of the population) by the year 2000 (Campodonico 1993; Chauvin 1995; EFE 1995; Morley 1995).

In light of such statistics, Guillermo Cook, a Methodist theologian who has worked and taught in Latin America, has expressed great pessimism that Pentecostal Protestantism can be a significant step to overcoming poverty in the present economic situation of Latin America. He states:

Although Protestants continue to appeal to the mystique of di-
vinely ordained upward mobility, in actual fact, working-class and
peasant Protestants are finding it increasingly more difficult to sub-
sist, let alone to prosper. In fact, an increasing number of lower-
middle-class Protestants are also becoming impoverished. The
trend is noticeable, even in a country such as Costa Rica, which
not too long ago was considered to be fairly prosperous. Protestants
are joining the ranks of the unemployed and dispossessed. Increasingly one finds dirt-poor Protestants facing the same problems as
their far more numerous Catholic neighbors. They are being forced
out of their rented houses in the working-class suburbs, or being
pushed off of their small plots of land into the growing *barrios
marginales* that fester around the major cities of the region. . . .
(Cook 1994a, 151)

The problem with some of the expectations that Pentecostalism
will act as a similar modernizing force in Latin American economies as it has in some North Atlantic countries is that the macro-
economic conditions are quite different in late twentieth-century
Latin America from those in England in the eighteenth century
and the United States in the nineteenth century. England and the
United States during those eras were both beginning a process of
labor-intensive industrial growth that, despite some inhuman working conditions, at least offered employment opportunities to large
numbers of poorly educated and unskilled workers. Immigration to
the United States was also a possibility for workers in England and
on the continent. With both industrial jobs and opportunities in
the vast unsettled lands of the West, the United States offered new
opportunities for those poor who were inspired by a work ethic,
Protestant or not. Moreover, the welfare state on the continent and
the New Deal in the United States occurred after such changes were
underway and acted to improve working conditions, to secure the
gains already made by hard work, and to assist those not able to take
advantage of such opportunities.

When Emilio Willems conducted research in Chile and Brazil in
the early 1960s reform democratic regimes were in place beginning
a process of land reform and increased social services for the poor.
Capital-intensive industry was not nearly as widespread as it is now,
and tariff barriers still protected labor-intensive manufacturing. His
optimism about the advantages of a work-oriented Protestant ethic

benefiting poor persons in such a context was reasonable (Willems 1967).

None of these conditions exist in Latin America at the present time, nor do current economic strategies by governments facilitate their emergence in the foreseeable future. The type of industrialization that is the most dynamic today in Latin America and that is supported by foreign investment is more capital-intensive than labor-intensive. The employment that expanding industries offer is primarily for those with skills. Many of the traditional industries that hire the unskilled (clothing, shoes, food processing, beverages) are going out of business due to reduced tariff barriers and the importation of cheaper comparable goods from abroad. In the countryside, ample unused and arable land is not available. Agrarian reform has stalled in many countries due to resistance by large landholders who still wield considerable political influence. The small landholders who produce food for the domestic market are being driven from their lands due to foreclosures in the light of an influx of imported food products from abroad. Large capital-intensive estates which grow cash crops for export are replacing them. Thus, there are no frontiers to which the poor can go to gain free arable land, even for those who have a strong work ethic and who are risktakers.

Immigration barriers in Europe and the United States put migration abroad out of the question for most of the poor in Latin America. The reduction of social spending and deregulation of private enterprises by governments reduce chances that the state will cushion the impact of increasing poverty among the majority of citizens. The welfare state has existed in varying degrees in all Latin American countries since the 1930s (as it has in the United States) but is being rejected as counterproductive for the free market system just at a time when poverty is deepening, not declining. The type of unrestricted capitalism now underway in Latin America has not been seen for over fifty years and the likelihood that it will be gradually "tamed" by expanding job opportunities for the unskilled and increased social legislation and services by the state is very unlikely for quite some time.

David Martin is optimistic that some of the successes discovered by Willems two generations ago will be multiplied now that Pentecostalism has grown so significantly since that time. He believes that

Pentecostalism is breaking the "monopolistic Catholic culture" in Latin America (which he views as patriarchal and says inculcates passivity) and is creating a "free social space" in which values of voluntarism, fraternity, and solidarity may provide a powerful stimulus to socioeconomic development (D. Martin 1990, 278–81). He wisely cautions that significant change may take "two or three generations" and that successes will depend on Pentecostalism's ability to continue its expansion among the masses and its "ability to advance their condition" (D. Martin 1990, 232).

Aside from his stereotyping of Catholic culture (which for the past two generations has been undergoing significant change itself from the social commitments of bishops, lower clergy, nuns, and lay activists), Martin does not address adequately the complexities of the current economic landscape throughout the region and how it is different from eighteenth-century England or nineteenth-century United States. Currently, Latin America shares few economic similarities even with its own situation thirty years ago, or with Europe and the United States one to two centuries ago that managed to pursue both economic growth and social equity amidst expanding industrialization. Cultural changes are important to lay the groundwork for successful structural changes in society, but the outcome of cultural and economic interactions will differ from one context to another if there are significant structural differences. The likelihood that the cultural changes underway from Pentecostalism will lead to the same upward mobility for the poor in Latin America as Methodism and Pentecostalism did for their respective followers in England and the United States is questionable without some important changes of direction in economic policies and models now being implemented (Berryman 1996, 176–79).

3. Incubators and Legitimizers of Political Authoritarianism

There is a body of literature that is pessimistic about the political implications of Pentecostalism. Some view it as a paternalistic refuge from the secular world breeding passivity and dependence (Lalive d' Epinay 1969, 1975; Bastian 1990, 1992, 1993; Kamsteeg 1991) and believe that it tacitly, or openly, supports authoritarian political regimes with which it shares ideological similarities (Lalive d'Epinay 1969, 1975; Bastian 1990, 1992, 1993). There are three different arguments underlying this position: (1) religious communities with hierarchical authority patterns are by nature antithetical to democratic values; (2) denominations that tend to be sectarian keep their members from participating in the organizations of wider society; and (3) Pentecostal denominations are supportive of authoritarian political regimes that mirror their own strict internal patterns of control.

The first argument (stressed very much by Bastian) may be true under certain conditions, but not always. Catholicism traditionally has been characterized by hierarchical patterns of religious authority and, in fact, Church leaders were suspicious of modern democratic movements in the eighteenth and nineteenth centuries. The main reason was the anticlerical tone of many of the early European proponents of democracy and their attacks on Church privileges in society. This was also true for nineteenth-century Latin America where Liberal and Radical parties were opposed by the Church for their efforts to separate Church and state (Mecham 1966).

The Vatican, as well as bishops in Latin America, in the early part of the twentieth century, however, came to see forms of democracy as much more compatible with Christian values and protective of Church interests than Communism, Fascism, and Nazism. They encouraged Catholic laity to form Christian Democratic parties in the 1930s and 1940s. In Europe (especially in Germany, Italy, and France) these were important contributors to post–World War II economic and political reconstruction. In several countries of Latin America during the 1960s and 1970s these parties supported socioeconomic reforms favoring the poor and acted as a moderate counterbalance to extremism on both the left and the right (Fogarty 1957; Fleet 1985). Although Christian Democracy is not as politically competitive in Latin America as it was a generation ago, Catholics are found in parties supportive of democratic processes across the political spectrum and few support extremist movements wanting to restrict democracy.

Pentecostalism shares some of the characteristics of Catholicism in the sense that pastors exercise strong leadership over their congregations and expect strict allegiance to their doctrinal and moral teachings. Nevertheless, there is much more active participation by laity in religious ritual than is true even in post–Vatican II Catholicism. The strong sense of community solidarity, affirmation of individual dignity, and emotional support given to each person by pastors and fellow believers alike does not encourage passivity in one's personal life but rather a critical reevaluation of one's moral priorities and goals. The sense of joy in experiencing the Lord's presence in one's spirit can be exhilarating and enable one to face up better to challenges in one's personal or family life. None of these values or experiences undermine the basis for democracy, despite the control patterns exercised by pastors.

Moreover, some studies of the internal dynamics of Pentecostal communities indicate that pastor-disciple relationships, although hierarchically structured, can lead to creative initiatives by laity, including many nonministerial roles for women. The gifts of the Spirit are theoretically open to all and lay specialists in healing, prayer, spiritual counseling, and missionary work can emerge unpredictably and spontaneously with no specialized training or certification by clergy (Drogus 1997, 59–61; Williams 1997, 187; Froehle 1997, 210). Spirit-filled laity can also branch out to form new communities, becoming pastors themselves for these new groups. Hence, the system is not so tightly controlled as to prevent personal initiative and new leadership roles (Kamsteeg 1991, 105–12).

David Martin may be closer to the truth than is Jean-Pierre Bastian in viewing these local authoritarian patterns in a wider context of positive religious experiences, and therefore as not being seriously debilitating for independent and critical thinking in the long term. He argues that "safe enclosures" led by strong protective leaders can be environments in which personal confidence, a sense of peace, an awareness of one's self-worth, and ability to serve others can be restored among persons who do not have much hope in their lives. Moreover, sometimes out of such religious contexts that seem to act as havens from the world, new social ideals and energies to reform societies can emerge—as happened with monastic communities in the Middle Ages with the Bohemian Brethren, as well as the Mennonites and the Quakers in modern times (D. Martin 1990, 286–88).

Michael Dodson, drawing upon the insights of de Tocqueville, makes a similar point about the long-term contributions to Latin American democracy that Pentecostal communities can make. By creating through vital private associations an "equality of condition" where individual self-worth and initiative can flourish,

Dodson argues, Pentecostalism will solidify the basis for democratic society (Dodson 1997, 28–31).

The Latin American Catholic Church itself is a more recent example where a vertically orchestrated institution created within its ranks local communities that helped stimulate some creative religious ideas with important social and political significance (Christian Democracy in the 1930s, 1940s, and 1950s, and liberation theology in the 1960s and 1970s).

Even more telling evidence of the antidemocratic implications of Pentecostalism is that many of its churches had offered legitimacy for authoritarian regimes in Latin America in the 1960s and 1970s. In Brazil after the military coup in 1964 the Presbyterian Church underwent a serious split with Evangelicals and Pentecostals taking control, purging political progressives from the ranks of leadership, and offering moral legitimacy to the new regime (Alves 1985). A decade later Pentecostal pastors in some areas of the country were openly courting favors from local government officials who were members of the official party of the military government (Hoffnagel 1978).

In Chile, after the September 1973 military coup, many prominent Pentecostal pastors made public statements in support of the military. Later, in December 1974, several thousand Pentecostals enthusiastically welcomed General Pinochet who participated in the inaugural ceremony of their recently completed immense "Protestant cathedral," Jotabeche, in Santiago. This was just two days after 2,500 Protestant pastors and laity (predominantly Pentecostals) had expressed their unconditional public support for the military government (Puentes Oliva 1975; Lalive d'Epinay 1983; D. Martin 1990, 240–41; Cleary and Sepúlveda 1997, 105).

In Argentina, after the military takeover in 1976 that began a reign of repression, most Pentecostal church leaders remained silent. They also did not participate in ecumenical efforts by some mainline Protestant and Catholic lay groups to defend human rights. Some even openly sided with the military (D. Martin 1990, 245).

In Guatemala, during civil wars in the 1980s, similar patterns were evident. Pentecostal pastors, invited by the government of General Ríos Montt (a Pentecostal himself), settled in areas where the army was establishing "strategic hamlets" against guerrillas and carried out significant relief activities (assisted by American

Evangelical groups) in close cooperation with government agencies (Garrard-Burnett 1986; Schafer 1992, 219–31; Stoll 1993, 167; Brouwer, Gifford, and Rose 1996, 56–57). Pentecostal churches became so identified with the Guatemalan military during the mid-1980s that they acted as safe havens from army persecution and grew most rapidly in war zones (Garrard-Burnett 1986, 217; Stoll 1993, 174–79).

Moreover, there is ample evidence of Pentecostal theological statements and sermons of pastors downplaying the importance of involvement in social and political organizations. Instead, their focus is on changing individuals' personal morality and they support the improvement of relationships with family and friends as the preferable means of alleviating societal injustices (Peck 1984, 191–96; Rolim 1985; Valverde 1990, 78–81; D. Martin 1990, 258; Berryman 1994a, 207–9, 211–15).

There is evidence, however, that points in a different direction and shows that not all Pentecostal pastors support political authoritarianism, nor do all followers engage in social escapism. In the 1970s, Brasil para Cristo, one of the largest Pentecostal churches in Brazil with 450,000 members, was known for its opposition to military repression. Its leader, Manoel de Mello, openly praised Catholic bishops for their criticisms of human rights violations and chided the Brazilian Protestant Federation for its silence on this front (Stoll 1990, 320; D. Martin 1990, 258–59). Regina Novaes, in her study of Assembly of God Pentecostals in Pernambuco, Brazil, in the early 1980s, found that a significant number of its members joined rural labor organizations in order to prevent the loss of their small plots of land to large dairy farmers (Novaes 1985, 152–53). Cornelia Butler Flora's study of Pentecostals in Colombia in the early 1970s indicates that, although not in the vanguard of political action, they will not oppose groups they see as acting for the best interests of their neighborhoods and will participate in community actions to improve living conditions in their respective areas, such as water strikes, protection of prisoners, etc. (Flora 1976, 87, 227).

John Burdick's study of Pentecostals in the municipality of Duque de Caxias just north of Rio de Janeiro in the 1980s found a similar pattern as discovered by Flora in Colombia: Pentecostals working in factories are reluctant to involve themselves in unions, but do not oppose strikes, and, in fact, can be counted on to remain loyal to union objectives if strikes remain peaceful. He also discovered that Pentecostals do join community organizations such as renter associations and peasant unions in areas with newer, more heterogeneous populations where Catholics have not already taken over the leadership positions. They also provided up to 10 percent of the progressive Workers Party (PT) membership in the region since it was recently established and free from the taint of corruption that plagues so many of the established parties in Brazil (J. Burdick 1993a, 206–22, 1993b, 25–26, 32–35).

Rowan Ireland found in his study of Assembly of God denominations in Campo Alegre in the 1980s in northeast Brazil that some Pentecostals associated with poorer, less institutionalized churches held views very critical of injustice and corruption and were willing to get involved to help out persons victimized by local officials (even when their pastors held different views). A small minority were also allies of members of Catholic CEBs supporting land invasions. Members of older, more established Assembly of God communities whose members had more stable employment were less willing to engage in such activities and agreed with their pastors who associated with local political elites (Ireland 1991, 93–108; 1993, 49–62).

Heinrich Schafer found in Nicaragua significant socioeconomic differences among Pentecostal churches that had political implications. Those with members of higher income were much more likely to oppose the Sandinista regime, whereas members of those among the poor were willing to cooperate in the social projects of the leftist government (Schafer 1992, 194–206).

Even within the same region, time and context makes a significant difference for Pentecostal social and political involvements. David Stoll found in his study of the northern Quiché region of Guatemala that Pentecostals who had shunned social involvement during the civil war had become more visible in community affairs after the conflict subsided in the late 1980s by starting new businesses, organizing cooperatives, and even running for public office (Stoll 1993, 194).

In reverse, Steigenga and Coleman in their study of opinion surveys of Protestants over time in Santiago, Chile, found that during the Allende regime in 1972 they were more supportive of Allende (30.6 percent) than Catholics (27.4 percent) and a substantial percentage identified themselves as politically on the left (41 percent) with only 18 percent placing themselves on the political right. After seventeen years of military rule (1973–1990), however, in 1991 in Santiago none expressed identification with the left, 40 percent had no political identification, 44 percent believed the military should have stayed in power longer, and a significant number felt the military were guilty of only some, or no, human rights abuses (60 percent). Many also believed that the military had done well in fighting crime (66.7 percent), reducing social inequalities (40 percent), guaranteeing a free press (40 percent), and supporting democracy (35.6 percent) (Steigenga and Coleman 1995, 471, 475–78; Tennekes 1978).

In Central America, throughout the civil wars of the 1980s, there was a minority of Pentecostals as individuals or factions who actively supported leftist movements. By 1981 there were enough Guatemalan Pentecostals involved with the guerrillas to form an autonomous auxiliary organization called the Confraternidad Evangélica de Guatemala (Garrard-Burnett 1986, 209, 217). A number of Pentecostal churches participated as members of the Evangelical Committee for Development Aid (CEPAD) which maintained cordial relations with the Sandinista government in Nicaragua and cooperated in government-sponsored projects to assist the poor (Saenz 1994, 197–98). A small, but significant, number of Evangelical and Pentecostal communities in El Salvador, Guatemala, Honduras, and Nicaragua also collaborated with local Catholic base communities in offering assistance to those persecuted by right-wing military organizations in the 1980s (Cook 1994a, 154; 1994b, 128–30; 1997, 85–86; Fried and Gettleman 1983, 230–31; Spykman *et al.* 1988, 221–22).

What all of the above evidence indicates is that important distinctions must be made within Pentecostalism now that it has become a significant part of the population in Latin America. Diversity exists and it is not possible to treat the movement as a monolith politically, even within the same country or region. Pastors' views (which tend to be more conservative) must be distinguished from the attitudes of rank-and-file members, not all of whom are the same in their political outlook (J. Burdick 1993b, 29). The organizational level of churches and the socioeconomic status of members affect political attitudes and behavior of members. Pentecostals in newer churches with less organization and poorer Pentecostals (who are the majority) sometimes are willing to engage in political action challenging the status quo. Those residing in the countryside about to lose their small farms seem more willing to act politically to defend their land than those recently arrived in urban slums with no property (Hoekstra 1991, 52–56). When a political context discourages political opposition to the government, Pentecostals may retreat strategically or even give their support to a military regime, but in open democratic contexts they seem more willing to participate politically, sometimes even on the left.

Since the late 1980s there have been signs that Pentecostal leaders are coming to recognize the importance of addressing the larger structural problems which continue to plague the continent and to take more outspoken positions in favor of social justice. In March 1989, in Buenos Aires, 129 representatives of twenty-nine Pentecostal churches from different Latin American countries met at the Latin American Pentecostal Conference (EPLA) to discuss common concerns, including the issues of poverty and exploitation. They called for a new approach to their ministry—a "contextualized evangelization"—whereby they would go beyond a focus on the individual to include a demand for change in "specific structures which produce poverty, misery, and avarice" in society. They affirmed that the Church must announce the reign of God's justice but also testify to such justice in its own life here and now (Schafer 1992, 211–12).

In August 1992, the Third Latin American Congress on Evangelization (CELADE III) took place in Quito, Ecuador, where more than 1,000 Protestant pastors and theologians convened. This was the first time that the Latin American Council of Churches (CLAI), representing the mainline Latin American Protestant churches, met with the Latin American Evangelical Confraternity (CONELA), a federation of the major Latin American Pentecostal denominations The final document issued from the joint meeting acknowledged that the Latin American Protestant Church as a whole has not sufficiently exercised a sense of social responsibility but has often "isolated itself from social and political processes," and in "some cases it has even justified violent dictatorial regimes." The statement, supported by mainline Protestant and Pentecostal church representatives alike, concluded that "the church must affirm the life denied by all sin, by unjust structures and by avaricious interest groups" (Cook 1994b, 125–26).[1]

The Latin American Theological Fraternity (FTL), an organization that had a major input into the preparation of the CELADE III conference, has been working since 1970 to facilitate dialogue and cooperation between historic Protestant churches and the newer Pentecostal denominations throughout Latin America. Headquartered in Brazil, but composed of theologians from mainline churches from several Latin American countries, FTL is characterized by a theology that is conservative on issues of biblical interpretation, the importance of personal prayer, and the need to work for conversions—which has given it credibility in the eyes of many Pentecostal pastors—but it does emphasize the need for all Protestants to be a force for social justice in their respective societies. FTL helped to convince a number of Pentecostal leaders of the importance of this issue and organized a series of consultations on theology and social problems in the early 1990s (Freston 1994, 235–41; Cook 1994b, 135–37).

In the 1960s, when liberation theology was emerging in the Catholic Church, some of the mainline Protestant churches in several Latin American countries moved to the left theologically and politically. In countries such as Chile, Brazil, Bolivia, Paraguay, and Argentina ministers and lay leaders from the Lutheran, Methodist, and Presbyterian churches joined in ecumenical human rights committees with Catholics to defend those suffering from repression under military governments (B. Smith 1979). Earlier continental-wide Latin American Conferences on Evangelization were dominated by those from historic churches who favored the positions espoused by liberation theology (Montgomery 1980). Such words and actions frightened many Pentecostals who feared that the mainline Protestant churches were making the same mistake as Catholics—overinvolvement in social and political issues to the detriment of preaching the gospel and deepening the spiritual life of laity. FTL has avoided becoming associated with liberation theology and political activism, and, as a result, has been an important bridge builder between the historic Protestant churches and Pentecostals. This has resulted in a greater openness by some Pentecostals to listen to its message about the importance of Protestant public prophecy on behalf of justice (Freston 1993, 102–4).[2]

As a striking example of this emerging social commitment by Pentecostals, Everett Wilson illustrates their educational network in

El Salvador. There the Pentecostal Centro Evangelístico now supports a network of private schools, the Liceo Cristiano, with 24,000 students on thirty-four campuses throughout the country. This network also includes basic medical and dental care and supplementary welfare services for its students and families. It is also being duplicated by Pentecostals in other Latin American countries, and, although some financing is coming from international Pentecostal sources, the driving influence and control are local (Wilson 1994b, 19).

There is also an emerging awareness among many Pentecostal leaders that they need a solid intellectual formation if they are to treat societal issues with a serious ethical perspective. In the past several years pastors from the mainline churches have been invited to visit and preach in Pentecostal churches, and professors from some of the divinity schools run by historic Protestant churches have been invited to teach at Pentecostal Bible institutes that are now beginning to emerge. Some interdenominational divinity schools of the mainline churches which are respectful of Pentecostal doctrine, such as the Seminario Bíblico Latin-americano in San José, Costa Rica, the Comunidad Teológica Evangélica in Santiago, Chile, the Methodist Institute of Theological Studies (IMET) in São Bernardo, Brazil, and the Latin American Faculty of Theological Studies (FLET) in Caracas, Venezuela, have all been attracting an increasing number of Pentecostal ministers in recent years. These ecumenical institutions provide courses in biblical studies, the history of Christian doctrine, pastoral counseling, and social ethics (D. Martin 1990, 251–52; Plou 1992; Gilfeather 1992; Berryman 1996, 175–76).

In addition to recent interest among some Pentecostal pastors in preparing themselves to address social issues effectively, some Pentecostal laity have become active in party politics now that military regimes have been replaced by democracies throughout Central and South America since the mid-1980s. In Brazil in 1986 the thirty-three delegates elected to the 500-member constituent assembly, created to write a new constitution after twenty-one years of military rule, were Protestant, and eighteen of these delegates were Pentecostals. The "evangelical bench" consequently became the third largest caucus in the assembly (Freston 1993, 73; Berryman 1996, 174). In the 1990 Brazilian elections twenty-nine Protestants were chosen as deputies and senators, seventeen of whom were from Pentecostal churches. A "pro-Collor" Pentecostal movement during that campaign helped elect political independent Fernando Collor to the presidency on a platform that promised an end to corruption and support for public morality (Freston 1993, 82, 85; Padilla 1994, 83; Serbin 1997, 10).

In the 1990 presidential elections in Peru political independent Alberto Fujimori and his Cambio 90 movement made explicit appeals to the Pentecostal vote by promising an end to corruption in government, a solution to the mounting violence of the guerrilla movement Sendero Luminoso, and effective solutions to rampant inflation and a stagnant economy. Many believe the Pentecostal vote helped him win the presidency along with his second vice-president, who was a Pentecostal, and twenty congresspersons on the Cambio 90 ticket who were also Pentecostals (Merino 1990, 1; Arroyo and Paredes 1992; Freston 1993, 67). A few months later the first Protestant president in Latin America was elected in Guatemala, Jorge Serrano Elías, a member of the "El Shaddai" neo-Pentecostal Church—although the Pentecostal vote does not seem to have been the decisive factor given his broad support across several sectors of society (Padilla 1994, 83, 88; Hallum 1996, 106–10).

These electoral successes helped stimulate Pentecostal political interest. Between 1980 and 1994, twenty-four parties with close ties to Protestant (particularly Pentecostal) churches were created in eleven Latin American countries: Argentina, Bolivia, Brazil, Chile, Colombia, El Salvador, Guatemala, Mexico, Nicaragua, Peru, and Venezuela (Cook 1994b, 131; Steigenga 1995, 1; Williams 1997, 192; Froehle 1997, 217–18; Bastian 1997, 103). The leadership for these movements is coming primarily from the neo-Pentecostal denominations that have experienced growth beyond the working classes into the middle and upper-middle sectors of society. Those who have offered themselves as political candidates are frequently pastors, lay leaders who are active in their churches, and close friends or relatives of pastors (Freston 1993, 99; Padilla 1994, 89–90). In some of these countries, such as Bolivia and Venezuela, Pentecostal candidates have also chosen to compete for office within secular parties so as to spread Pentecostal influence across the political spectrum and thus maximize impact on public policy (ALC 1997; Froehle 1997, 217).

Research on Brazilian Pentecostal politicians in the late 1980s and early 1990s has shown some interesting patterns. Three of the six major Pentecostal churches in the country have made a conscious decision to run candidates for office (the Assemblies of God, the Church of the Four Square Gospel, and the Universal Church of the Kingdom of God). The clergy often handpick candidates, church leaders orchestrate the Pentecostal vote so as to minimize competition among Pentecostal candidates and maximize the support for each, and a Protestant caucus now meets regularly in congress (Freston 1993, 83–86). There is no overarching political ideology that characterizes the position of these newly elected leaders, nor do they have a group of intellectuals to advise them (as do the Catholic CEBs with their well-trained clergy) nor an elaborate social doctrine (as do the Catholics).

The specific issues that are uppermost on the agenda of these newly elected Pentecostal officials in Brazil include: (1) a return to honesty in government; (2) prevention of any legislative reforms that would threaten Pentecostal positions on family values (e.g. legalization of abortion, further liberalization of divorce laws, legal recognition of rights for homosexuals, government-funded campaigns to stop the spread of AIDS by encouraging safe sex) and the backing of laws supporting family values (censorship of the printed and electronic media and stiffer penalties for the use and sale of drugs, both aimed to protect children); (3) the protection of full religious liberty for all churches by removing legal privileges for the Catholic Church (favored mention in the Constitution, public subsidies to Catholic schools); and (4) the promotion of material benefits for their respective churches and a recognition of their societal importance by government (Freston 1993, 100–102). Some of these rapidly growing churches, especially the Universal Church of the Kingdom of God which has 3.5 million members, are becoming particularly skillful in pursuing this last objective and have obtained from government special favors for themselves, such as free television time on publicly owned channels (Serbin 1997, 10).

It is also clear, however, that Pentecostal politicians in Brazil are not enthusiastic about the neoliberal economic model that is exacerbating the conditions of the working classes. In voting on economic policies in the late 1980s, according to trade union scoring, Pentecostal politicians rated higher in support of workers' interests than the constituent assembly as a whole, and considerably higher than the elected representatives from the mainline Protestant churches. Although in the middle classes, these Pentecostal representatives are well aware that the vast majority of Pentecostals who vote for them are not as successful as they are. Hence, they are willing to vote in support of measures to alleviate poverty (Freston 1993, 88–89, 91).

Research on Pentecostal political objectives in Nicaragua (where several parties associated with various Pentecostal churches have been formed in recent years) reveals some similarities with the Brazilian patterns. Political leaders from these churches have as their foremost objectives: (1) the protection of equal rights for all persons, including the right to life for the unborn; (2) a complete separation of church and state, with an end to public subsidies for Catholic schools and to the requirement that Catholic doctrine be taught in public schools; (3) greater controls on public officials to prevent corruption; (4) the promotion of a formal dialogue between churches and the state to help eradicate poverty, promote public morality, and reconstruct the social and economic fabric of the country (after prolonged civil tension between Sandinistas and their opponents) (Zub 1994, 7–8).

In the October 1996 general elections in Nicaragua, the recently created Pentecostal Nicaraguan Christian Path (CCN) party came in third, gaining 4.1 percent of the national vote behind the victorious Liberal Alliance (51 percent) and the runner-up Sandinista (FSLN) party (37.7 percent). Although its percentage of the vote was small, CCN surpassed twenty other political parties and now can play a broker role in forming coalitions if the two leading parties cannot hold all their members in line on controversial legislative votes (Jeffrey 1996a, 7; Zub 1996b, 2–4).

There is now an international Latin American Union of Evangelicals in Politics which is trying to promote dialogue and coordination among all Protestant elected officials throughout the region. The organization was formed at a conference in Buenos Aires in October 1991 attended by sixty Protestant politicians, political scientists, pastors, and theologians from sixteen countries representing various religious and political orientations from left to right. Pentecostals were well represented at this meeting, along with the Latin American Theological Fraternity (FTL) and the Brazilian

Evangelical Association (AEVB). Conservative Evangelical church groups from the United States also attended the meeting, including Pat Robertson's Regent University, the Providence Foundation, and the Rutherford Institute—all of whom supported a type of "dominion theology" for Latin American Protestant politicians that would promote Christian values in public life and reconstruct society along biblical principles. The meeting did not, however, issue any strong calls for Protestant criticism of social injustice or the economic models exacerbating it, but rather called for an International Christian Alliance of Political Parties and Movements that would include conservative Catholics from the Catholic Charismatic movement (discussed below) who share many of the same concerns with Pentecostals in wanting to promote family values through public policy initiatives (De Powell et al. 1992; Cook 1994b, 131; Freston 1993, 91; Froehle 1997, 217).

Thus far it is too early to predict the trajectory of these new political movements and strategies of Latin American Pentecostals. Despite some electoral successes, there have been significant disappointments. None of the Pentecostal parties have yet received significant percentages of the electoral vote in any country. Some of the presidential candidates whom Pentecostals have helped to elect have not lived up to expectation. Fernando Collor of Brazil resigned from office in the face of impending impeachment for misuse of public funds. Poverty in Peru has increased since Alberto Fujimori became president in 1990, and he also suspended constitutional freedoms and closed Congress in 1992 in order to fight counterinsurgency more effectively. High officials (including the president himself) in the administration of Jorge Serrano Elías of Guatemala displayed the same tendency for luxurious living and unwillingness to attack government corruption as his predecessors, and he disbanded the Congress and the judiciary in mid-1993 to prevent investigations into fraud in his administration. Several of the Pentecostal representatives in the Brazilian constituent assembly were accused in 1988 of trading votes for favors for themselves or their churches (C. Smith 1991, 139; Freston 1993, 77; Padilla 1994, 92–94; Williams 1997, 192–94).

Various public opinion surveys conducted in the early 1990s throughout Central America indicate political behavior and attitudes among rank-and-file Pentecostal believers that may have an important bearing on the future successes of newly formed religious parties and politicians closely associated with churches. The majority are poor with less income and education than most Catholics (Coleman et al. 1993, 113–16). They are voting in large numbers, normally at the same high rate as Catholics—averaging in the 70 percent levels in Central America in the early 1990s (Stein 1992, 28; 1995; Williams 1997, 191). In some countries (e.g. Costa Rica), Pentecostals vote at an even higher rate than members of mainline Protestant churches (Steigenga 1995, 18–19). Church affiliation has little to do with party affiliation in Central America, with Pentecostals as diversified as mainline Protestants and Catholics—with the exception that Pentecostals showed a considerably higher degree of approval for Guatemalan Pentecostal president Jorge Serrano Elías than did Catholics in 1993, and Pentecostals in Nicaragua in 1991 were overwhelmingly supportive of newly emerging Pentecostal parties (Stein 1994, 8; Zub 1993, 102).

Central American Pentecostals tend to be aware of and sympathetic to concerns of the lower classes, such as increasing poverty, continuing violence and human rights abuses (even under civilian governments), and the lack of accountability of politicians (Williams 1997, 190). Some are also active in community organizations, such as parents' associations and other community self-help associations, that are using peaceful and nonconflictual strategies to alleviate the most immediate problems in their areas (Bautz 1994, 64, 82). In Guatemala, fundamentalist Protestants (most of whom are Pentecostals) in a 1993 national survey even appeared more willing to engage in various forms of communal or civic participation than Catholics or those with no religion (Seligson and Jutkowitz 1994, 90–91).

Pentecostals also tend to exhibit a higher degree of approval of their respective governments and political systems than do Catholics (Coleman et al. 1993, 124; Stein 1994, 12; Steigenga 1995, 20; Williams 1997, 192). They are less willing than Catholics to take part in public actions or movements to redress grievances that are confrontational—such as land invasions and public protests involving civil disobedience (Stein 1992, 22; Stein 1994, 13; Bautz 1994, 73; Bowen 1996, 206–7)—and they are uncomfortable with church leaders acting as mediators in social and political conflicts (Coleman et al. 1993, 126).

These surveys throughout the six Central American countries also found that those Protestants who identified with fundamentalist religious views (support for a literal interpretation of the Bible, belief that only Christians can gain religious salvation, a conviction that punishment is more characteristic of God than mercy towards sinners) to be considerably more on the right in party affiliation, more supportive of the social and economic status quo, and much less tolerant of the rights of politically unpopular minorities (Steigenga 1995, 23; Stein 1992, 34). Although fundamentalism cuts across denominations, it is more prevalent among Pentecostals than among historic Protestants and Catholics (Stein 1994, 34).

Finally, opinion surveys in Chile in 1990 and 1991 showed Pentecostals to be quite conservative on issues of family morality as these are affected by public policy. Chile is now the only country in Latin America where divorce is not legal, despite many out-of-wedlock unions and considerable bribery of officials to grant civil annulments on technicalities. Nevertheless, over three-fifths of Pentecostals (62.9 percent) are against the legalization of divorce. More than eight of ten (82.3 percent) are also against the legalization of abortion, and almost one-half (45.5 percent) are against contraception to limit births. In addition, nearly three-fifths (57.7 percent) support government censorship of morally objectionable cinema (Fontaine Talavera and Beyer 1991, 95–99).

What all this recent evidence on Pentecostals entering into party politics and the polling of Pentecostal political behavior and attitudes indicates is that rank-and-file Pentecostals do not fit some of the stereotypes that have been used to characterize them politically (Dodson 1997, 35–36; Williams 1997, 194–97). They are not in principle apolitical, nor are they always supportive of reactionary political regimes. They are now participating in a whole spectrum of communal associations and political parties throughout Central and South America, and in several countries have created parties of their own to compete in elections. Newly elected Pentecostal politicians are not supportive of policies that favor large business or landed interests nor those of U.S. corporations; rather they favor modifying current economic policies to alleviate the sufferings of the poor. Some rank-and-file Pentecostals engage in peaceful community action to improve the immediate quality of life in their communities. A small minority may even be willing to go further and engage in more controversial actions, such as land invasions and collaboration with Catholics in defense of human rights when they are threatened.

It is also clear, however, that thus far the majority of Pentecostals are still leery about political involvement beyond voting and many decline to participate in community organizations in which they are not dominant. Those who have ventured into political leadership roles (predominantly from the middle classes) also lack an ideology to inform their choices other than a desire to make society reflect biblical values (Berryman 1996, 174–75; Hallum 1996, 111–12). They often do not have the intellectual underpinnings to articulate a social ethic that is comprehensive and flexible enough to guide them and other policymakers (including non-Pentecostals) facing complex political, economic, and social problems. Many are concerned about reducing poverty, but there is little indication as to what specific measures they will support if their political influence increases.

Moreover, Pentecostal politicians (and other politicians Pentecostals have supported) have not always lived up to promises given before elections (e.g., to fight corruption). In each country studied where they have entered politics, they are clearly concerned with reducing Catholic Church privileges in law and preventing any legislative reforms that would tolerate greater pluralism in the area of sexual morality throughout society. Although they would find allies in other denominations who share some of these concerns, these commitments are not conducive to the formation of wide-based political coalitions. Neither are Pentecostals supportive of public policy decisions reached by consensus if the moral values they hold as absolute are at stake.

3

ASSESSMENT OF
CONTEMPORARY CATHOLICISM

Despite considerable and sustained efforts by the Vatican throughout the 1980s to pull the Latin American Catholic Church back from
intense social and political commitments, both the hierarchy and
those involved in local base communities have not significantly curtailed their involvement in public issues. The bishops throughout
the region have continued to be outspoken on policies they consider to have serious moral implications for both Church and society
and, in several countries in the 1980s and 1990s, have offered their
mediating services to resolve conflicts between government and opposition. Local Church leaders engaged in the creation and guidance of small communities have continued to spend a considerable
amount of time and resources on serving the wider social and economic needs of their respective neighborhoods.

What is clear, however, is that some of the issues the bishops have
chosen to address in their public statements have changed, reflecting
both a new political context with the return to democracy and the
new religious and moral emphases being stressed by Rome. There is
also now considerable heterogeneity among base communities, with
some focusing much more on spiritual issues than on social activities
and only a minority including both a religious and social emphasis
equally.

Episcopal Pronouncements and Strategies

There has been no decline in Episcopal statements and actions on
various public policies despite the growing number of theologically
conservative bishops in every Latin American country. The public issues which have most preoccupied the hierarchy are economic
and political justice, legislative proposals of newly constituted

democracies dealing with issues of sexual morality (divorce, abortion, sex education, birth control, methods of preventing the spread of AIDS, rights for homosexuals), and the protection of Catholic Church interests in the face of growing religious pluralism in society.

(1) Social Justice. In the 1980s bishops in several Latin American countries were instrumental in helping to bring about a return to civilian rule and the reestablishment of constitutional democracy acceptable both to the military and to civilian politicians. In addition to being among the first groups willing to speak publicly in favor of a return to democracy, bishops often were instrumental in promoting dialogue between military officers and their civilian opponents to negotiate the terms of redemocratization.[1]

In some cases (Brazil and Chile) bishops helped to strengthen a consensus among civilian party leaders so that they could negotiate more effectively with the military on the terms of disengagement. In other countries in the 1980s (El Salvador, Nicaragua, and Guatemala) and in the 1990s (Mexico, Peru, and Colombia) bishops acted as mediators between government and guerrilla leaders to work out cease fires, lay the groundwork for an end to insurrection, or to negotiate the release of hostages (Ross 1994; Fleet and B. Smith 1997, 111–12; Chauvin 1997a and b).

In Argentina in early 1997 some bishops helped to mediate between government officials and groups from poor areas mounting angry public protests against economic policies. On occasion they successfully stopped the use of repressive police force against the demonstrators (Plou 1997).

Now that democracies have been reinstated in almost all Latin American countries (Cuba being the exception), the hierarchy has continued to speak out on what they consider necessary issues in order to maintain such regimes on a sound moral basis. This has entailed addressing what the bishops consider to be the unfinished human rights agenda and the necessity to guarantee equity in the process of economic restructuring.

In some countries (Chile, El Salvador, and Guatemala) the hierarchy as a group has called for a full disclosure of human rights abuses under past military governments and the identification by name of those responsible for such crimes. Although this is a very sensitive political issue and newly established democratic regimes do not want to risk the ire of military officers recently returned to the barracks, the bishops in these countries believe that amnesty is only meaningful from a moral point of view if culpability is acknowledged. No effective national healing can take place, they argue, until responsibility for past atrocities is identified and the culprits own up to their actions.

In Guatemala the bishops have gone so far in their pursuit of knowledge about past human rights abuses as to establish a Truth Commission to investigate the political violence that took place during thirty-five years of military rule. Not trusting the objectivity of the study conducted by the government, the bishops authorized a massive publicity campaign encouraging victims of violence to come forward to be interviewed by local church workers about details of the abuses they suffered. Archbishop Próspero Penados del Barrio of Guatemala City stated in 1995 that only through such an impartial and complete investigation will the "silence imposed by fear" be broken. He also claims that "peace is only possible when there is repentance, recognition of guilt, and pardon" (Jeffrey 1995).[2]

Both at the continental level through the Latin American Episcopal Conference (CELAM) headquartered in Bogotá and at the national level through various episcopal conferences, bishops have issued continual denunciations throughout the 1980s and early 1990s about what they consider to be the severe social costs of economic policies being pursued by newly established democratic regimes.

The fourth general assembly of the Latin American Episcopal Conference met in Santo Domingo in October 1992, and Pope John Paul II participated along with bishops representing every country throughout the continent. The Vatican played a much more aggressive role in setting the agenda and selecting the presiding bishops and theological advisers than in previous general assemblies of CELAM held in Medellín, Colombia (1968) and Puebla, Mexico (1979), since it wanted issues such as Church unity and discipline and the central religious nature of the Church's mission emphasized. The final document issued at the end of the two-week conference reflected these concerns in its section on christology and ecclesiology, but it also included sections that addressed critical economic issues facing Latin America today and affirmed the Church's continuing role in promoting social justice (Hennelly 1993).

The document of CELAM IV at Santo Domingo condemned current neoliberal economic strategies that are geared "to deregulate the market indiscriminately; to eliminate important parts of labor legislation as well as laborers' jobs," and "to reduce social expenditures that protect workers' families." The bishops also questioned whether third-world countries should continue to pay off debts to foreign banks and governments (over $400 billion in Latin America alone by the early 1990s) if to do so will seriously jeopardize the quality of life for the majority of their people (Peerman 1993, 182).

The document also reaffirmed the Church's "preferential option for the poor . . . as solemnly proclaimed at Medellín and Puebla" and renewed its commitment to defend the human rights of all citizens. It also gave the Church's full moral support to forms of democracy that are "pluralist, just and participatory"—implying that merely formal democratic processes, such as party competition and open elections, are insufficient to provide an adequate definition of what bishops consider true democracy to be (Richard 1992, 16–18).

Subsequent statements by CELAM after the 1992 Santo Domingo meeting further illustrate the continuing willingness of the Latin American bishops to speak out on economic and political issues. In March 1993 the annual meeting of CELAM's Council criticized economic neoliberalism, this time for making "economic success more important than human beings" with the end result that "people pay for its mistakes." The seventy bishops on the Council also warned officials in newly established democracies that they were failing in their social responsibilities to alleviate poverty, thereby causing mounting frustration among the poor:

> Various democratically elected governments have only brought frustration to the citizens who elected them. This, in turn, makes many people distrustful and insecure. Governments change, the parties and the leaders in power change, but the situation remains the same, and in some cases becomes worse. (Cosgrove 1993b, 1)

A report issued by CELAM in May 1995 predicted that the current free-market economy being implemented across the continent will collapse because it is "unnatural and inhuman." The report also pledged the Church's commitment to use its moral and financial resources to fight extreme poverty, rising unemployment, violence, and corruption that plague so many Latin American societies today (IPS 1995, 2).

National episcopal conferences of bishops in several countries have articulated a similar message about their displeasure with some of the economic and political policies of their respective governments. In their first collective statement after the severe restrictions on the Mexican Church by the Constitution of 1917 were relaxed in 1992, and while the government was priding itself in its image of creating a modern economy, the bishops warned that poverty had reached intolerable levels in Mexico, causing a "grave crisis of social inequality" and creating in reality two Mexicos—one "immense, hungry and underdeveloped; the other small, rich, modern and international." They also criticized the North American Free Trade Agreement (NAFTA), one of President Salinas's showcase projects, for not sufficiently attending to the needs of internal markets and consumer demands in Mexico ("Mexico" 1993, 8; Camp 1997, 69). After 1995 when the Mexican economy began to experience serious recession, episcopal criticisms of government policies have increased and even politically conservative bishops have spoken out sharply on these issues (Ross 1996, 12).

The Venezuelan bishops have issued several pastoral letters and statements in recent years on what they consider to be failed government policies adversely affecting the poor. They have criticized rising unemployment, indecent housing, elite control of policymaking (despite the formal trappings of democracy), and electoral fraud (Cleary 1989, 313–29; Lee 1992, 1–2; Cosgrove 1993a, 4).

In 1994, amidst numerous strikes and worker takeovers of factories protesting drastic wage cutbacks and the relaxation of health and safety regulations in factories, the Uruguayan bishops rejected government claims that social unrest was being orchestrated by subversive elements. They blamed the current austerity measures being imposed by the government's neoliberal economic strategy. They stated that economic life must be governed not only by efficiency but by ethical norms that guarantee both the "legal security of economic interests" and the "demands for social justice" (Blixen 1994, 3).

The Ecuadorean episcopal conference in April 1993, after a 40 percent decline in the standard of living in six months, issued a similar call for the injection of moral concerns into economic planning.

They declared that the "modernization of the state goes much further than the privatization process" and requires the construction of an "economy of solidarity" which can "satisfy demands of justice" ("Ecuador" 1993).

In April 1997 the Episcopal Conference of Brazil (CNBB) strongly criticized the government for chronic delays in implementing its promised agrarian reform. They also accused the administration of President Cardoso of buying votes in the Congress to gain a constitutional amendment allowing him to run for a second term. They also took the government to task for not prosecuting assassins of landless peasants (Tautz 1997).

Although not offering specific policy solutions for problems of growing poverty amidst economic restructuring, Latin American Catholic bishops are clearly pointing to what they consider the moral illegitimacy of unrestrained free-market activities that place unbearable costs on the poor. Even theologically conservative bishops are willing to sign such statements since they are in keeping with the century-old tradition of papal social encyclicals calling for restraints on capitalism for the sake of the common good, including state regulations on business and public provisions of social services to alleviate inequities among classes.

Pope John Paul II in his own encyclicals on social problems has reiterated these same themes of the responsibilities of private property and the necessity of state intervention in the economy to protect the most vulnerable in society. In several trips to Central and South America he has repeatedly called for more humane public policies to reduce poverty.

In some countries (Brazil, Bolivia, Guatemala, Mexico, and Argentina), in fact, high government officials have openly criticized bishops for what they consider to be undue interference in complex economic issues by those with no competence in these areas. There is no indication, however, that either the pope or the conservative bishops he has been appointing in Latin America consider their repeated public criticisms of economic policies as overstepping their moral responsibilities to preach the traditional social doctrine of the Church in the face of massive poverty aggravated by free decisions of those with power.

(2) Personal Morality. The second area where bishops have been outspoken has been sexual morality. The legislatures in several of

the newly constituted democracies have proposals under considera-
tion that would liberalize laws in this area and which are drawing
strong criticism from the Church hierarchy.

Chile is the only country in the hemisphere that still does not
legally recognize divorce, but it does grant annulments if legal ir-
regularities can be proven in the performance of marriages. This
has led to innumerable cases of bribery each year by the wealthy to
have public officials find some "mistake" in original marriage li-
censes while thousands of poor live in concubinage since they cannot afford the $300 "cost" of such proceedings. The legalization
of divorce has been introduced in the Chilean Congress to remove
such inequities, but it has been blocked by leaders of the Christian
Democratic Party (many of whom are relatives or close friends of
bishops). The episcopal conference has repeatedly denounced efforts
to change the current law, arguing that although there are "painful situations that affect married couples" divorce laws "only add to
the further dissolution of the family" and thus are "contrary to
God's law and the good of the nation" ("Chile" 1990; Meehan 1991;
Cabieses 1994). The bishops have also publicly opposed a change
(already approved by a committee in the House of Representatives) that would legalize homosexual relations between consenting
adults and remove sodomy as a crime from the Chilean Penal Code
("Chile: No Homosexuals, Please." 1995).[3]

In all Latin American countries, except Cuba, abortion on demand is illegal. In some countries it is permitted under limited circumstances, such as rape, serious threat to the life of the mother,
and deformation of the fetus, and sometimes only after such conditions have been proven in court. In Brazil, for example, abortion
can be performed legally when a judge deems that rape has occurred
or the life of the mother is in jeopardy. Under such restrictions, this
means that legalized abortion is not available in most cases. As a
result, it is estimated that between 10 and 12 million illegal abortions
occur in Latin America each year (most under unsafe conditions),
with anywhere between 6,000 and 50,000 women dying and close
to a million more hospitalized with post-abortion complications
(Simons 1988; IPS 1997, 4).

There are feminist movements in several Latin American countries that have grown in size and outspokenness since the return to
democratic government, and these women are demanding changes
in the legal system to make abortion legal and affordable to all. In

some countries in the early 1990s (Argentina, Costa Rica, the state of Chiapas in Mexico), proposals have, in fact, been introduced in legislatures to legalize abortion.

In each case, the Catholic bishops have strongly opposed such reforms as being contrary to Church teaching. The same CELAM Council meeting in 1993 that criticized leaders of democratic governments for aggravating poverty by their economic policies also denounced the killing of abandoned street children (by police and vigilante squads in Brazil and Colombia) and "in their mothers' wombs." Equating both actions as attacks on children, the bishops argued that "killings cannot be legalized" (Cosgrove 1993b, 1).

The bishops in Costa Rica sharply criticized a proposal introduced in the legislature in 1991 to legalize abortion in cases of rape or incest, arguing that adoption is the Christian and humanitarian solution to unwanted children. They also opposed new sex education textbooks being used in public schools as incompatible with a Catholic moral perspective on sexuality. The government acquiesced to the bishops' request by making the recommended changes (McPhaul 1991).

When a bill was introduced in the Argentine legislature in 1990 to decriminalize abortion in cases of rape, nearly all the bishops stated their opposition, and Catholic lay groups from the upper classes aligned themselves with the hierarchy in criticizing the proposal. The bishops also announced that they considered family planning as a "step toward abortion" (Plou 1990; 1994).

In 1993, when a new national constitution was being written, the Peruvian episcopal conference mounted a campaign (unsuccessfully) to include in the document provisions prohibiting abortion and sterilization. The Church also collected 50,000 signatures asking the government to stop promoting the use of contraceptives in its public health clinics and to adopt in its place the Church's approved program of natural family planning based on the Billings method ("Peru" 1993).

The Vatican has supported the Latin American bishops in their opposition to both abortion reform and artificial methods of birth control. The Vatican is also using its own direct access to Latin American governments through the offices of papal nuncios to pressure presidents and congresspersons to oppose legalized abortion. During preparations for the International Conference on

Population and Development held in Cairo in September 1994 the papal nuncios lobbied hard and won the support of the governments of Guatemala, Nicaragua, and Honduras to oppose any mention of abortion at the meeting. Two months before the Cairo conference, President Carlos Menem of Argentina, in deference to the Vatican, proposed an amendment to the Argentine constitution guaranteeing "the right to life from the moment of conception" ("Latin America" 1994; Plou 1994).

The spread of AIDS and the virus (HIV) that causes it has become another preoccupation of public officials in Latin America. The number of reported cases of AIDS in the region has increased from 8,000 in 1987 to nearly 60,000 in 1993. The increase is generally attributed to unprotected bisexual behavior by Latin American males and, as a result of irresponsible male behavior, a growing number of women (especially wives) are becoming infected with the disease or its related virus. In Brazil there are now an estimated one million people infected with HIV, with an additional 225,000 in Mexico and 200,000 in Colombia (Brooke 1993, A1).

Governments in several countries (Brazil, Mexico, Colombia) have taken aggressive measures to stop the spread of AIDS with education programs in the schools and campaigns on public television promoting the practice of safe sex. The Catholic Church in both Brazil and Chile has also opened special hospices to care for victims of the disease, sometimes despite stiff opposition from residents near such buildings who fear contagion (Martins 1989; Frasca 1989, 7). However, in both Colombia and Mexico, the bishops vigorously protested television ads promoting the use of condoms as a way of preventing the spread of AIDS and its related virus. In both instances, the respective governments withdrew the advertising from television (Brooke 1993, A5). A conservative Catholic lay organization in Mexico, Pro-Vida, has supported the bishops' position and also has charged that the government's promotion of condoms to stop AIDS is actually being directed by large multinational corporations interested in profits (Frasca 1989, 2).

If conservatives in the Vatican and in the Latin American episcopacy can defend their critical stance on economic issues in light of traditional Church teachings about social morality, they can do the same for their public opposition to laws proposing changes in acceptable sexual morality. As in the areas of economic equity, par-

ticipatory government, and respect for human rights, so too on issues of abortion, birth control, and the limitation of sexual activity
to marriage, there is a long-standing Catholic tradition that prelates feel morally obligated to defend in public. The difference between the two areas is that, thus far, Latin American bishops have
been more successful in gaining governmental compliance to their
wishes on the second moral agenda (sexuality) than on the first (eco-
nomics).

(3) Defending Catholic Interests vis-à-vis Pentecostalism. The final
area that has preoccupied Catholic bishops has been the privileged
position the Church still enjoys in most Latin American countries
(in law and in numbers) and the challenge to this hegemony presented by Pentecostals.

Due to the growing religious pluralism in society, Catholicism's
spiritual monopoly is steadily declining. An increasing number of
Catholics, as described earlier, are turning to Pentecostalism. In addition, those who describe themselves as having no religious identification are on the rise. As a result, pressures are being exerted
on lawmakers, both by Pentecostals (as mentioned earlier) and by
the religiously nonaffiliated, to complete the separation of church
and state and thus remove some of the vestiges of Catholic privileges that still exist in law in several countries, such as subsidies to
Catholic schools, special mention of Catholicism in national constitutions, and the teaching of Catholic doctrine and morals in public
schools. The Catholic bishops are using their influence, however, to
block such measures from being implemented. In some cases, they
are even pushing elected officials to increase these privileges or to
place legal restrictions on non-Catholic churches to curb the spread
of Pentecostalism.

In Bolivia, for example, the constitution declares that "the state
recognizes and sustains the apostolic Roman Catholic religion."
In 1992 the National Association of Evangelicals (ANDEB)—upset
at what it considered stringent controls on non-Catholic worship—
collected 24,000 signatures supporting a proposed constitutional
amendment separating church and state and recognizing all denominations equally before law. The official newspaper of the
Catholic Archdiocese of La Paz, *Presencia,* denounced the petition.
The editorial accused the signers of being a mixture of Marxists and

"certain sects of eminently Anglo-Saxon origin" whose goal was to "weaken the principal historical and cultural thread that Latin America possesses in Catholicism." It also claimed that the amendment, if passed, would weaken the social integration of Bolivia. The proposal has not proceeded beyond committee in the legislature, and it is expected to take several years to pass given the political influence the Catholic Church still enjoys (Dave Miller 1992).

In both Argentina and Ecuador, Catholic bishops are pushing to have Catholic religion classes included in the curriculum of public schools (something which already exists in some other countries, such as Colombia and Chile). There is stiff opposition by the school teachers' union to this proposal in Ecuador, and in neither country (partly because of the additional costs to be incurred by the state) have the bishops been successful in their efforts. The Evangelical Fellowship (a federation of major Protestant churches) in Ecuador has also vigorously objected to the bishops' proposal, arguing that "the law would transform our educational institutions into centers of discrimination" (Coppola 1992, 4; Collins 1994, 2).

In Nicaragua, the Minister of Education, a conservative Catholic with close personal ties with Cardinal Obando y Bravo of Managua, in early 1997 suggested new textbooks for use in government-mandated religion courses in public schools. In these books the pope and the Virgin Mary were both extolled and Protestants were warned not to treat either with disrespect or else they will "pay heavily." Protestants were also blamed for racial discrimination in the United States against African Americans and indigenous peoples. Pentecostal pastors reacted strongly to this bias and argued that such government-subsidized materials violate the constitution that indicates the state has no official religion (Jeffrey 1997).

In Paraguay there is discussion underway in the government to reduce the annual public subsidy to the Catholic Church. The government provides the Church each year with $400,000 to help pay salaries of teachers in Catholic schools and to defray the administrative costs of the Paraguayan episcopal conference. The bishops have been earnestly negotiating with the government to prevent this subsidy from decreasing. Their argument is that the Church is fulfilling a mission of service to society and deserves state aid for its work ("Paraguay" 1993).

Catholic bishops have also continued to criticize Pentecostal churches publicly. The 1993 CELAM Council document which denounced current neoliberal economic models in Latin America placed some of the blame on Pentecostal denominations (referring to them as "sects"):

> There is not only an interest in evangelizing behind the sects; important economic interests are looking for religious support. These sects become an instrument for ideological domination, to prepare the terrain for the application of economic models imported from the United States. (Cosgrove 1993b, 1)

In a 1992 pastoral letter entitled "Protestants and Sects," the Chilean bishops spoke deferentially about the mainline Protestant denominations but warned against what they perceived to be the negative impact of the "sects" (Pentecostals, Jehovah's Witnesses, and Mormons) on the Catholic Church. The growth of these groups, they claimed, has led to "confusion and doctrinal disorientation" among Catholics as well as "family divisions" and a "feeling of inferiority" in face of the "pressure of proselytization." They also claimed that the "sects" were guilty of a "lack of respect for religious symbols and images of the Catholic Church" (Conferencia Episcopal de Chile 1992, 42).

In both Argentina and Chile, Catholic bishops want the state to impose legal registration requirements on all non-Catholic churches due to the increasing number of Pentecostal denominations in both countries. In Nicaragua, Protestants have criticized the government of President Violeta Barrios de Chamorro, a devout Catholic, for religious discrimination by providing state money to the Catholic Church for its new cathedral in Managua and for granting tax exemption to all Catholic institutions, while levying taxes on some of their own activities, including the large Baptist hospital in the capital city (ENI 1994; Serbin 1992, 406).

In order to compete better with Pentecostals, the bishops have decided to adopt some of the Pentecostals' own strategies. There is currently underway throughout the region two official Catholic evangelization projects, Lumen 2000 and Evangelization 2000, aimed at keeping additional Catholics from converting to Pentecostalism. Subsidized in large part by Catholics from Europe and the United States, these projects involve both media and door-to-door campaigns to reach those Catholics who do not regularly attend Mass so as to bring them into a closer relationship with the Church (Plou 1991, 7).

The Brazilian Catholic Church, for example, is currently setting up a new national Catholic television station called "Life Network," with the assistance of some Brazilian media owners. Given the good relations some bishops maintain with wealthy Catholic business and media experts, the station will be allowed to use the Brazilian Tele-communications Company satellite and thus reach the whole country with its programming. An estimated $50 million is being invested in the operation, and it is hoped by the end of the 1990s that it will be the largest Catholic TV operation in the world. Its purpose is to compete more effectively with Pentecostal churches that are now increasingly using the media to spread their own message (Rocha 1994).

In addition to greater reliance on the media to evangelize, bishops have also been increasingly emphasizing the importance of the spiritual formation of lay Catholics at the grassroots level. The general assembly of CELAM that met in Santo Domingo with the pope in October 1992, in addition to reaffirming the Church's commitment to social justice, called for the multiplication of small communities and movements of laity who would participate in the spiritual mission of the Church. This "new evangelization" singled out for special mention women and youth as having important roles to play in the life of these communities, especially in catechesis (teaching of religion to children), celebration of some rituals, and in missionary work to spread the Catholic faith (Richard 1992, 19–20; Alvarez Gandara 1992, 57–59).

Episcopal conferences in several Latin American countries throughout the 1980s also affirmed the importance of increasing spiritual vitality at the local level of the Church. Bishops in Brazil (1982), Bolivia (1986), and Chile (1989) all reaffirmed the critical role of ecclesial base communities (CEBs) in the formation of laity with commitments both to social justice and to a deeper understanding of the Catholic faith. The bishops of Colombia dedicated themselves to a renewal of the sacramental life of parishes and acknowledged the invaluable support lay people give in maintaining the spiritual life of the Church in areas where priests are unavailable (Cleary 1989, 43–66, 72–81; Conferencia Episcopal de Chile 1989).

The Chilean bishops, in their 1992 pastoral letter, "Protestants and Sects," called for the training of Catholic lay activists in a greater understanding of the Bible and of Catholic doctrine. They also urged these lay leaders to act as neighborhood missionaries (using the same face-to-face and door-to-door contacts employed by Pentecostals) to get nominal and fallen-away Catholics to return to an active participation in the Church's life (Conferencia Episcopal de Chile 1992, 72–78).

The Guatemalan hierarchy (1986) recognized the positive role the Catholic Charismatic movement is playing in the renewal of the spiritual life of laity in that country. This movement shares several of the characteristics of Pentecostal Protestantism since it emphasizes an outpouring of the Holy Spirit experienced through personal and communal prayer, speaking in tongues, and physical and spiritual healings. Although the bishops saw some dangers in the movement if not properly guided by priests, they were generally positive in their assessment and encouraged it to continue within the boundaries of the Church (Cleary 1989, 67–71).

The Brazilian bishops in 1994 publicly voiced similar support for the Charismatic movement, provided it remain closely linked with Church authorities (Serbin 1997, 12). It has been growing in several other Latin American countries as well, especially in dioceses where bishops or priests have given it their personal blessing (Williams 1997, 197, 200). It has also received cautious but clear Vatican endorsement that is concerned about its remaining under clerical supervision (Hallum 1996, 88–90).

All of these efforts by the bishops over the past decade have been to protect the privileges of the Church in Latin American societies and to make it more spiritually competitive with the increasing numbers of Pentecostal churches today (sometimes by borrowing from some of the pastoral strategies of Pentecostals themselves). While these efforts by the hierarchy may seem reasonable from the point of view of a defense of traditional Catholic interests, many of the tactics the bishops are using are not conducive to improving relationships with Pentecostal churches which they still view as their enemy.

Characteristics of Catholic Activists

If the bishops—including the conservative prelates appointed since the return to democracy—have not reduced their interest in societal problems, neither have Catholic activists at the local level. Just as there is a diversity of public policy issues preoccupying the hierarchy, priests, nuns, lay leaders, and rank-and-file members of base communities (CEBs) have continued to be engaged in a variety of social as well as religious activities.

The continued outspokenness of the hierarchy about issues of social justice has been matched by continuing Church sponsorship of programs to alleviate poverty at the regional and local levels throughout Latin America. International Catholic social service agencies, such as Catholic Relief Services (CRS) in the United States, the Canadian Catholic Organization for Development and Peace (CCODP), the Campaign against Hunger and Disease in the World (MISEREOR) in Germany, the Central Agency for Joint Financing and Development (BILANCE) in the Netherlands, the Catholic Fund for Overseas Development (CAFOD) in Great Britain, and the Catholic Committee against Hunger and for Development (CCFD) in France all continue to collect money from Catholics in their respective countries and send it to both diocesan and local Catholic groups in Latin America for relief and development projects.[4]

Catholic Charities (CARITAS) organizations in each diocese use this aid to sustain health and nutrition projects for needy persons, emergency assistance for victims of natural or human-made disasters, shelters for the homeless, orphanages, and, more recently, hospices for those affected with AIDS. Priests, nuns, and lay leaders active in base communities receive some of this relief assistance to support nutrition and basic health programs at the local level along with rehabilitation services for alcoholics.

There is also a network of small-scale development projects that local church activists sponsor throughout the continent which address the longer term causes of poverty rather than only alleviate some of its immediate effects. Local church groups now support, with international assistance, revolving loan funds for small business persons who are too high of a credit risk for commercial bank loans. Rural parishes have created buying and selling cooperatives for small farmers so as to cut out the exorbitant prices often charged by middle agents. Local church personnel have also undertaken the task of developing water systems for drinking and irrigation in remote rural areas not served by public or profit-making institutions (B. Smith 1990, 241–54, 271–75).

There is no evidence that any of these relief and development projects have been curtailed with the appointment of a new generation of bishops. Poverty has worsened, not declined, with the return of democracy in Latin America over the past decade. Even theologically conservative bishops have judged such programs as consistent with the Church's official commitments to social justice and to a preferential option for the poor in its ministries.

It is also evident that the institutional Church in Latin America (with substantial foreign assistance) has continued to sustain controversial programs to assist those who are still victims of injustice despite the return of formal democracy. Some Church-sponsored human rights organizations (originally created during the era of severe military repression or civil war) continue to operate. This is particularly the case in Central America where human rights violations continue to occur, albeit at diminished levels than a generation ago. The recent commitment by the Guatemalan bishops to create their own fact-finding organization to investigate past abuses against civilians is an indication of the extent of the Church's continuing commitment to human rights in some countries (Jeffrey 1995).

The Brazilian episcopal conference through its Indian Missionary Council (CIMI) continues to support programs to assist indigenous people being evicted from their lands in the Amazon. Its Pastoral Land Commission (CPT)—staffed by priests and lay persons—remains in the forefront of the movement to implement agrarian reform legislation. Some Brazilian priests associated with this organization live under threats from death squads supported by absentee landowners who resist the Church's call for an equitable distribution of unused land to the poor (Bruneau and Hewitt 1992, 50–53; Adriance 1995, 69–70; Rocha 1995).

Hence, there are continued involvements by local Church personnel in areas of poverty alleviation and struggles for social justice, even if some of these efforts are politically controversial. What has changed, however, is that open confrontations between local Church leaders and bishops have become less frequent since the return to democracy, and some of the more extreme aspects of liberation theology widely discussed a generation ago are now quite rare.

Throughout the 1970s and early 1980s, when military governments were in power in most of the region and civil war plagued several countries (especially in Central America), local base communities of the Church were often havens for leftists persecuted by their respective governments. Some in base communities made the decision to leave CEBs and join revolutionary organizations to fight oppressive regimes. Christian-Marxist collaboration was tacitly, if not openly, encouraged by some priests and nuns supervising local Church communities, and the resort to violence as a last means of self-defense against oppression was accepted. These activities incurred the wrath of the military who harassed, expelled, and sometimes murdered, local Church personnel for such controversial tactics, thus reducing the already scarce pool of local pastoral leaders. Such tactics also brought local priests, nuns, and lay leaders of the CEBs into direct confrontation with their local bishops over disagreements about what were legitimate pastoral activities.

Much of this tension between local Church personnel and governments has disappeared since the return to democracy. The political demands on the Church have subsided now that civilian rule is in place. Not only have human rights violations declined but other opportunities for participation have opened up beside Church communities now that many of the restrictions have been removed on party politics and labor organizations. Those who sought refuge in local Church communities during military rule in Central America and the Southern Cone region now can pursue their social and political objectives better through secular organizations. The image of base communities serving as havens for the political opposition at the local level and the role of the bishops as being the major national voice of opposition to governments (as it clearly was in countries such as Brazil, Chile, Bolivia, Paraguay, Guatemala, El Salvador, and Nicaragua) are no longer accurate. The political role of the Church has become far less crucial as a defender of human rights and constitutional processes than it was in much of Latin America from the early 1970s through the mid-1980s (Stewart-Gambino 1992, 8–10).

Although some local Church activities in the areas of human rights, land reform, and the protection of indigenous peoples are still considered controversial by some—both in governments and wider society—they are within the legitimate scope of Church concerns in the light of official Church social pronouncements. Bishops are more willing to tolerate local Church leaders pursuing these objectives than involving themselves in partisan political movements or directly or indirectly abetting insurrectionary activities.

Liberation theologians have continued to write about the need for Latin American Catholics to include a serious commitment to social justice within their faith commitments, but they have downplayed some of the more extreme options endorsed a generation ago, such as collaboration with Marxists or the use of violence as a last resort to achieve social change (Crahan 1992, 178). In recent years, many of them have been stressing in their writings—as are the bishops—the necessity to expand the meaning of formal democracy beyond elections and elite-controlled party competition. They are urging policymakers to include support for expanded popular participation in decision-making and more effective government efforts to reduce poverty during a transition back to free market economies (C. Smith 1991, 230–32; McGovern 1989, 186, 589).

Moreover, much of the research that has been done on the characteristics of local base communities in different Latin American countries throughout the 1980s and early 1990s indicates that religious activities are far more of a concern to participants than political issues. Ted Hewitt's study of CEBs in São Paulo, Brazil in 1984 and 1988 found a gamut of different types of communities ranging from those purely spiritual in focus to those whose members were politically active. He also found that, looking at all of the CEBs in his survey together, more people participated in religious programs and the various church-sponsored charitable services than in activities aimed at raising political consciousness or in community action programs working for the social and economic improvements of their respective neighborhoods. Most CEBs were becoming "mini parishes," with the focus of the energies of leaders and members concentrated on prayer, Bible study, and the celebration of the sacraments (Hewitt 1991, 46–47, 93).

In his study of CEBs in Duque de Caxias (just north of Rio de Janeiro) in 1987 and 1988, John Burdick found a similar pattern. Members expressed far more interest in spiritual issues than social or political problems in their area. Lay leaders (a minority in comparison to rank-and-file members of CEBs) showed a higher rate of participation in non-Church related organizations, but these tended to be community movements aiming at the improvement of facilities affecting their immediate quality of life (land, electricity, schools) rather than political parties (J. Burdick 1993a, 183–203).

Daniel Levine's study of participants in local Church communities in several low-income rural and urban areas of Colombia and Venezuela in the mid-1980s found a great variety of emphases ranging from "highly pietistic and devotional to socially activist." Nevertheless, even in those groups whose members were involved in civic organizations spiritual issues were not neglected, since "in all instances there is great stress on prayer, Bible study, and liturgy." He also found that politics plays only a minor role in their concerns, since politicians are regarded with great distrust among the poor in both countries. Those CEB members who do engage in social action normally do so through Church-sponsored programs or in those community organizations which focus on improving the material condition of their own or their neighbors' daily life:

> Typical activities include sewing, visiting the sick, or "social action," which usually means collecting money, clothing, or food for those in extreme need. There are also commonly attempts to found cooperatives, which generally remain limited to very small-scale savings and loan operations or, at most, to collective marketing or common purchase arrangements. (Levine 1992, 49)

Phillip Berryman in his early 1990s study of local Church groups in Guatemala, El Salvador, and Nicaragua discovered that with a return to democracy there was a greater spiritual focus emerging in the pastoral ministries of the Church in several dioceses. Newer movements have sprung up among the urban middle classes alongside, or in place of, base communities, such as Catholic Charismatic renewal, Trigo (Wheat Ministry), and SINE (Integral System of New Evangelization). He observes that:

> The Catholic charismatic renewal, Trigo, and SINE have a number of evangelical-like features in common. All emphasize the Bible. . . . They see their primary role as evangelizing Catholics to the point where they accept Jesus as their personal Savior, and they propound a morality centered on the individual and the family. Yet their devotion to the Virgin Mary and respect for the pope mark them as distinctively and conservatively Roman Catholic. (Berryman 1994a, 168)

Some of these new groups are also using radio and television (e.g., Trigo in Guatemala) to reach fellow Catholics and keep them from leaving the Church (Berryman 1994a, 210–21). When Pope John Paul II visited Guatemala in February 1997 it was middle-class Charismatic Catholics and members of the neocatechumenate movement who stood at the front of the receiving line—not lower-class members of the dwindling CEBs (Jeffrey 1996a, 7).

Andrew Stein in his study of the Nicaraguan Church in the early 1990s found that the Catholic Charismatic renewal, SINE, the Legion of Mary, and the neocatechumenate (all with almost an exclusive focus on prayer and spiritual formation of laity) were more represented in parishes throughout the country than base communities (CEBs). In the past the CEBs have been associated with some partisan political movements or have experienced tensions with bishops over the proper mixture of religious and social involvement for official Church representatives (Stein 1995 ch. 3).

Edward Cleary in his study of the Guatemalan Church in the late 1980s found that even within the CEBs there was a greater spiritual emphasis than during the previous years of civil war. Lay members of CEBs are also now more aggressive in their door-to-door efforts to get nominal Catholics to return to the sacramental and prayer life of the Church and are beginning to have some success in their efforts (Cleary 1992a, 183–84).

Michael Fleet and I in our study of local Catholic organizations in Santiago and Lima in the late 1980s also found a variety of Church-sponsored religious groups (prayer circles, Legion of Mary, cursillo movements) coexisting side by side with base communities, all of which devote themselves primarily to spiritual activities (Fleet and B. Smith 1997, 242–43).

This evidence indicates that there is an overlap of some concerns between many local Catholic activists and the bishops in the contemporary Latin American Church. Social programs administered by priests, nuns, and laity to alleviate poverty continue to flourish at the regional and local levels, but there also has been a renewed emphasis on spiritual issues in various types of local Church movements (including within CEBs). In addition, there are the beginnings of a missionary spirit at the local level to win back lapsed and nonpracticing Catholics. All of these local activities parallel the official priorities endorsed by the hierarchy, including the newly appointed theologically conservative bishops. The last two priorities (spiritual formation and more lay involvement in evangelization) also parallel quite closely the characteristics of contemporary Pentecostal churches described earlier.

Since the return to democracy throughout Latin America, however, it seems to be true (at least in some regions) that the more one is engaged in the Church (regular Mass attendance and participation in one or more Church-sponsored local organizations) the less likely one is to join a social or political movement in the civic community. Ted Hewitt's (1991) and John Burdick's (1993a) research in urban areas of Brazil and Fleet and my (1997) surveys in Santiago and Lima all found this pattern to be true among local Catholic activists. Involvement in Church life seems to be all-consuming for many Catholic activists, and it is here where they feel most comfortable in creating an associational life. This again would parallel many of the findings of scholars who have studied Pentecostal behavior.

While some might conclude that this pattern undermines democracy by pulling people away from a concern with wider societal issues, it is important to point out that the research indicates that participation in CEBs has motivated, not detracted, at least some to become active in organizations seeking social change. Madeleine Adriance found in her study of CEBs in northeast Brazil that the majority of CEB members surveyed were also active in agrarian unions seeking land reform (Adriance 1986, 159; 1995, 67–69). Fleet and I also found that in Santiago a solid 20 percent or more of those active in local Catholic communities surveyed in low-income areas in the late 1980s were active in other neighborhood associations and were also members of political parties. In Lima 38.5 percent of local Catholic activists surveyed in poor areas also belonged to political organizations (Fleet and B. Smith 1997, 145, 239). Hence, as in the case of Pentecostals, sweeping generalizations about an aversion to politics by Catholic activists must be avoided.

Moreover, even those Catholic activists who are not members of parties or community organizations are sharing in experiences that are compatible with democratic values or processes. The types of behavior and attitudes being inculcated in these local Catholic organizations—both those that are primarily spiritual and those that include a social service component—are quite similar to those found in Pentecostal churches (which David Martin and others have argued are supportive of effective democracy over the long haul).

Daniel Levine's study of local lay Catholic activists in both Colombia and Venezuela found that they experience a growing sense of self-confidence in being able to handle the immediate problems of their daily lives more effectively. Participation in local Church groups has enabled individuals to cut down on drinking, treat their spouses and children with more respect, articulate their opinions in a group, and to develop a more caring attitude about their neighbors. In short, their self-image has dramatically improved and they are sensing a new ability to act and judge as independent agents who have something to offer their families and their surrounding communities. Levine concludes that this can have a profound long-range effect on democratic society, even if all of these people are not now engaged in political movements. Social change, he argues, comes about slowly, and shifts in attitudes and behavior that bring it about first occur in free social spaces not necessarily linked with political or civic movements:

> The development of a strong associational life provides underpinnings for a truly independent civil society. The resulting shift in popular culture from resignation, fatalism, and silent powerlessness to equality, activism, organization, and voice is a cultural and political change of major proportions. . . . Reference to supposed utopian hopes of turning the world upside down is neither realistic or necessary to explain and understand change. The popular voices raised in Latin America today have more modest goals and look to a surer foundation for the future.
>
> They want more dignity, better jobs, decent houses, and fair futures for family and community. They seek these ends by working in the open spaces made available by change elsewhere in the system. Once active, they can and do expand these spaces, making themselves into new women and new men in the process. (Levine 1992, 351–52)

As corroboration of this insight, Michael Fleet and I found that support for democratic processes was very strong among Chilean Catholic activists in lower and lower-middle class areas of Santiago during the final years of military rule when political dialogue was underway to effect a transition to democracy. About 90 percent in our surveys said they were interested in political issues, that parties were positive for democracy, and that the accommodation of class interests was preferable to the defense of one's own class. Almost 80 percent favored liberal democratic regimes that respected the rights of all, as compared to regimes that restricted both participation and other rights of some citizens. Three-quarters favored Christian-Marxist collaboration in rebuilding the democratic system of Chile (all leftist parties were then favoring a return to constitutionalism and none supported insurrection against the military). Moreover, approximately three-quarters identified themselves as having a leftist political tendency (Fleet and B. Smith 1997, 145, 184–86).

In Lima on some of these same issues Catholics involved in base communities, social service, or religiously oriented organizations scored lower in their support for processes of political accommodation and tolerance. Only one-quarter to one-third, for example, favored the accommodation of all class interests over the satisfaction of their own economic needs, and less than one-quarter felt that Marxist ideas contained any important political truths. Peru in the late 1980s had already undergone a transition back to democracy nearly a decade before Chile but was in the throes of severe political polarization and economic crisis. The Marxist terrorist movement, Sendero Luminoso, presented a serious threat to social order, and elected politicians seemed ineffective in solving any of these problems. Nevertheless, 60 percent to 70 percent of those surveyed expressed an interest in politics, about 70 percent still favored a liberal democratic regime that restricted no one's rights, 70 percent to 80 percent were optimistic that differences between rich and poor would eventually decline, and 80 percent to 90 percent identified themselves as being on the (constitutional) left politically (Fleet and B. Smith 1997, 239, 247–49).

This evidence is an indication that Catholic lay activists in newly established civilian regimes in Latin America—even if many do not participate in organizations beyond the realm of the Church—are not harboring attitudes subversive to a healthy democracy. They are neither politically radical (as feared by some critics of liberation theology), nor are they so preoccupied with religious issues as to lose all interest in politics or to accept authoritarian solutions to complex social problems (as some suspecting the Church of instilling reactionary tendencies had thought). They are political moderates who provide a reserve, or secondary, line of defense for liberal democracy and constitutionalism if these are placed in jeopardy by a resurgence of antidemocratic forces in the future. In sum, their political profile resembles in some ways that of Pentecostals.

Weaknesses and Latent Tensions in the Church

Despite these moderate political attitudes of Catholic activists and a rejuvenated spiritual emphasis in local Church ministries pleasing to the hierarchy, the number of committed Catholic laity the Church can count on to implement its religious and social agenda is still very small. Moreover, a commitment both to spiritual formation and social justice at the local Church level is not common among many laity. There are also a significant number of clerics who still want to preserve their authority and are uncomfortable with giving laity more autonomous roles in the Church's ministries. Finally, many Catholic activists and rank-and-file members do not agree with all the current priorities of the hierarchy, and although there is not yet open confrontation, latent tensions exist that could become more overt in the years ahead.

Despite the efforts by the hierarchy since the 1960s to expand the number of committed Catholics participating in the sacramental and organizational life of the Latin American Church, only a minority attend Mass regularly, and an even smaller number are members of base communities and other lay organizations. Approximately 85 percent of Latin Americans currently identify themselves as Catholics (about 380 million people out of a population of 450 million). The vast majority of these, however, are still only Catholic in name since they rarely attend Church. The rate of weekly Sunday Mass attendance varies from country to country, averaging between 15 percent to 20 percent (57 to 76 million), except in Mexico where Sunday observance is in the 40 percent range (Camp 1997, 114). The great majority of these "sacramental" Catholics are women and children since men do not attend Mass on a regular basis (Stewart-Gambino 1994, 133).

Those who are willing to do more than participate regularly in the ritual life of the Church and offer their time, energy, and sometimes resources, to the various religious and social organizations sponsored by the Church are even fewer. Ed Cleary estimates that there are approximately 20 million lay Catholics in all of Latin America (about 5 percent of the baptized) whose religious commitment is profound. They attend Mass faithfully and are also willing to devote their time to the Church's ministries (Cleary 1994, 206). It is from this group that the "organizational" Catholics come who participate in the various lay movements associated with the Church. Those who participate in local base communities (CEBs)—which have taken root primarily among the urban and rural poor and which attempt to combine both spiritual and social commitments— are even smaller in number, with some estimates as low as 3 million, less than 1 percent of all baptized Catholics in the region (Deiros 1991, 158).

Hence, the 40 million Pentecostals in Latin America are approaching the number of "sacramental" Catholics who attend Mass regularly. Some have even estimated than on any given Sunday now in Latin America there very well may be more Pentecostals attending church than Catholics (Stewart-Gambino 1994, 133), since almost half of Pentecostals in some countries attend Sunday worship weekly (Cleary and Sepúlveda 1997, 110). Many of these Pentecostals are also active in several of the other religious and social programs sponsored by their churches (attending church activities on the average of eight to ten times a month). Thus, the number of Pentecostal "organizationals" now may surpass the number of "organizational" Catholics (Stein 1992, 39).

The "cultural" Catholics (numbering in the range of 300 million) are those with the weakest ties to the Church, and it is among these Catholics that Pentecostals are making most of their converts (Cleary 1992b, 216; Berryman 1994b). The roughly 40,000 priests and 120,000 nuns throughout the continent cannot perform their current administrative, sacramental, and spiritual activities and also engage in significant new efforts to attract the "culturals" into a closer relationship with the Church. Some Catholic lay "organizationals" are starting to proselytize among the "culturals" (as mentioned earlier), but the number ratio (20 million attempting to reach 300 million) imply that their task is formidable. In addition, Catholic "organizationals" are already easily matched in numbers by the most committed Pentecostals who are busily fishing for souls in the same waters.

Moreover, there is not a well-established tradition of Catholic proselytization in Latin America. Catholicism has until recently enjoyed an overwhelming cultural monopoly and it has been a common assumption that even the nonpracticing are part of the Church. Over the past twenty-five years since they have been in operation local base communities, for example, have not engaged in such activities. They have normally waited for nominal Catholics to come to them for assistance or spiritual support rather than actively recruiting new members to their ranks. It will take some time to convince large numbers of lay activists to engage in door-to-door efforts to bring Catholic "culturals" into a closer association with the Church, which limits even more the Church's chances for competing with Pentecostals for their allegiance (Comblin 1994, 221).

In addition, there is a gap emerging between the spiritual ministries of the local Church—charismatic renewal, neocatechumenate, SINE, and Trigo—and its social service projects. Although official Church pronouncements signed by the bishops place equal importance on deepening one's religious commitment and working to alleviate the structural causes of poverty, there is more of a bifurcation between these two concerns rather than a synthesis in the attitudes and behavior of laity.

Phillip Berryman in the early 1990s found in Central America, and later in Brazil and Venezuela (Berryman 1996, 79–87, 116–19), that in discussions with local Catholic activists in Charismatic Renewal and Trigo there was a strong reluctance to discuss episcopal statements on the need for land reform or the work of local base communities who have tried to apply biblical teachings to contemporary social issues. Both priests and lay members in these new spiritual movements felt that concerns about structural inequities in society were beyond the scope of their ministries. They (like the majority of Pentecostals) expressed a conviction that working for a change of heart among individuals to accept Jesus as Savior is the best way to solve social problems. In fact, Berryman discovered in Guatemala that even alluding to the pastoral letters of the bishops on social injustice (which frequently cite the Scriptures), or mentioning base communities, evoked fears among these spiritually focused Catholics:

> In each of these conversations, simply mentioning the bishops' letter on land or Christian base communities triggered associations with violence. . . .

Thus, one set of church people sees a clear distinction between the gospel text and any kind of militant organizing, which is immediately linked to violence; the other set, representing not left-wing splinter groups but important sectors of the hierarchy, asserts that these same spiritual motifs are the foundation for a kind of pastoral work aimed at people's empowerment. (Berryman 1994a, 211)[5]

Even within CEBs themselves these divisions between the "prayers" and the "do-ers" often exist. Carol Drogus in her study of local Catholic women CEB activists in São Paulo in the 1980s found three types of members: (1) the "self-concerned or traditional religionists" interested in personal spiritual growth and improvement of family relations; (2) the "people-concerned religionists" who involve themselves in civic and political struggles for the betterment of their neighborhoods; and (3) the "integrated religionists" who combine an interest in spirituality with involvement in the charitable works of the Church. It is the second group—the "people-concerned religionists"—that provides leaders both for the CEBs themselves and some of the community organizations in their surrounding areas (Drogus 1992, 69–75).

In reflecting on the implications of her findings for the future trajectory of base communities in Brazil during an era when the bishops are emphasizing the importance of personal spiritual formation and family morality, she speculates as follows:

A resacralization of the CEBs and a renewed emphasis on domestic issues and family morality might prove an effective way to attract unaffiliated folk [cultural] Catholics, potential Protestant converts whom the CEBs have not reached. They would also be attractive to traditional religionists and at least some integrated religionists, two groups whose allegiance to the church is already fairly secure. These changes, however, would pose a different problem for the church. They would alienate the social justice activists who are the backbone of the CEBs, both religiously and politically. . . .

Having awakened many lay people to social activism through the CEBs in the 1970s and 1980s, the church has created its own dilemma for the 1990s. Strategies aimed at bringing folk Catholics into the sacramental fold and lowering the church's political profile are likely to alienate the very lay leaders the church created. Unless it can accommodate them and respect their independence and desire for a voice in the church as well as in society, the Brazilian church risks the loss of many of its hardest-working lay activists, particularly the women of the CEBs. (Drogus 1992, 81–82)[6]

This desire of lay leaders for a greater voice and independence is also frustrated by those clergy who want to maintain considerable control over the activities of base communities and other lay movements. José Comblin has described the "benevolent authoritarianism" that still characterizes some clerics in Brazil in their guidance of CEBs, especially in rural areas (Comblin 1994, 206–7). Ted Hewitt found in his study of CEBs in São Paulo a tendency for clerics and nuns to limit topics of discussion of CEBs, keeping, for example, issues such as birth control and abortion off the agenda (Hewitt 1991, 88–90).

Dan Levine in his study of the Colombian Church found that bishops and many priests try to maintain considerable control over all pastoral ministries, including local base communities. As a result, he concluded, there is much less chance for independent lay leadership to emerge—except in those regions under the pastoral guidance of the Jesuits, who by training tend to be more theologically liberal (Levine 1992, 74, 91, 211).

Andrew Stein in his study of the Nicaraguan Church was told by some bishops that many priests find it hard to adapt to the directives of Vatican II calling for the granting of more pastoral responsibilities to laity. What is surprising is that this seems to be more of a problem for younger clerics ordained in the last ten years. They seem to be very much taken with the social prestige of their position and are more concerned about exercising authority than many of the older priests who have greater pastoral experience and who are less preoccupied with clerical privilege (Stein 1995, chapter 3; 1997).

The seminary training of clerics today throughout Latin America has come under closer scrutiny by the Vatican (as mentioned earlier). This is resulting in a greater emphasis on the uniqueness of the priesthood in the light of scarce vocations and the continued resignation of active priests to marry. The Latin American Church as a whole has been quite successful in increasing the number of seminarians in recent years, with seminary enrollments increasing between 300 and 700 percent since the mid-1970s (Cleary 1994, 206). A by-product of this effort to make the priesthood more appealing, however, has been to reinforce its pre–Vatican II aura of being considerably above that of the lay person's vocation spiritually and socially. One result has been to attract an increasing number of young men into seminaries as much interested in the status of the position as in the service to others.

Some of the new recruits to the priesthood, because of this training and motivation, find it harder to work with lay persons as partners and to grant them an important voice in local Church decisions. This creates tensions between clerics and lay leaders, and some of the most creative and imaginative laity are not attracted to work under such tight controls.

Christian Smith has gone so far as to claim that efforts by Latin American clerics to reassert their control over lay groups in recent years could result in CEBs being "co-opted or domesticated by the legacy of monistic corporatism" whose "proven adaptability and durability" inside Roman Catholicism continues despite all the changes since Vatican II (C. Smith 1995, 9). This assessment may be too pessimistic, but there is evidence of growing differences of pastoral style between laity who take the reforms of Vatican II seriously and some newly ordained priests who prefer a traditional clerically controlled Church. These differences, if they continue, could lead to some serious tensions at the local Church level and the withdrawal from pastoral ministry (as Drogus predicts) of some very solid lay leaders.

A final serious problem facing the Catholic Church in Latin America in the years ahead is the latent tension between the bishops and laity (including the most devout) over some of the public stances that the hierarchy has taken in recent years. Both in the areas of economic justice and sexual morality there is considerable disagreement between what the hierarchy is calling for and what many Catholic lay people consider morally appropriate.

Despite repeated episcopal denunciations of current neoliberal economic policies underway throughout the region, and the bishops' call for adjustments to be made to alleviate the burden they are placing on the majority poor, no Latin American government has yielded to the Church's official voice on these matters. What is embarrassing is that most of those making decisions in governments are Catholics themselves—many "culturals," but in some instances regularly practicing who are on friendly terms with priests and bishops. The macro signs of economic health—declining inflation, increasing growth rates, growing foreign investment and trade—are seen by Catholic laity in decision-making positions as indications of the appropriateness of their policies. Their argument is that trickle-down benefits will occur for the poor over time. The bishops have been unable to convince these leaders of what they consider the immorality of sacrificing this generation of poor in the hope that the next might do better. As a result of this disagreement between the hierarchy and well-placed Catholic laity in government and business circles, the moderating influence of the bishops on economic policy-making has been minimal.

Some lay Catholics in the professional and business classes have heeded the bishops' calls for public Catholic opposition to changes in laws affecting either sexual morality or the legal privileges of the Church, but they have ignored the hierarchy's equally strong calls for more compassion for the poor in their economic decisions. This selective listening to the official voice of the Church by upper-middle and upper-class laity—noticeable during the 1970s when these same Catholics publicly rejoiced over episcopal criticisms of Marxism, while ignoring the hierarchy's denunciations of human rights violations by military governments which they staunchly supported—has continued under democratic regimes, albeit with different issues at stake.

Although the bishops have been successful thus far in blocking any changes in law affecting personal and family morality, there is evidence that large numbers of Catholics—including those who practice—do not support the positions of the hierarchy. In fact, the majority seem to favor liberalization in these areas.

In Brazil, the country with the largest number of baptized Catholics in the world (116 million), public opinion surveys have indicated that overwhelming numbers of Catholics do not obey Church teachings on family morality. A national survey in June 1994 of 2,076 adults revealed that 88 percent do not follow Church pronouncements on either birth control or abortion. In Brazil, for example, despite the fact that abortion is illegal, roughly the same number of abortions are performed annually as in the United States. Among women between the ages of 25 to 44, 90 percent indicated they do not comply with Church teachings in these areas. Despite the efforts of the Church to train health workers to teach natural family planning methods, it is not an appealing strategy to the vast majority of Catholic women. Two-thirds of married women are already using artificial methods of birth control due to the increasing pressures on the urban population to have smaller families. Fertility rates among women of childbearing ages in Brazil have dropped steadily from 5.8 children in 1970 to 2.3 children in 1994. This has largely been due to women using contraceptives, despite the hierarchy's successful lobbying effort to block legislation to make them available for free through Brazil's national health service (Brooke 1994, A1, A3).

Surveys done in Mexico in the early 1990s reveal similar patterns of lay dissent regarding official Church teachings on sexual morality. Seventy-four percent of Catholics favored family planning programs that involve contraception methods, and 50 percent approved of abortion in some circumstances. Moreover, 71 percent disapproved of the bishops' opposition to government-sponsored media efforts to prevent the spread of AIDS by encouraging the use of condoms (Camp 1997, 122).

In Peru, between the mid-1980s and the mid-1990s, the divorce rate tripled, and many women in both urban and rural areas are choosing to have fewer children. According to a 1993 UNICEF report, and a national survey taken by the Peruvian Health Ministry, about three-fifths of Peruvians are now using contraceptives (WFS 1994).

On similar issues polls in Chile have indicated that a significant number of lay Catholics are not in agreement with the current position of the hierarchy to stop the legalization of both divorce and abortion. An October 1989 survey of Catholic opinion, for example, indicated that only a bare majority (51 percent) of all Catholics favored keeping divorce illegal, which the bishops are demanding. Moreover, 62.4 percent of practicing Catholics who attend Mass regularly stated that they believed that divorce was justified when there was no longer love between spouses. On the issue of abortion, although 86.4 percent of all Catholics believed it is always a sin, 76.5 percent (including 70.9 percent of the regularly practicing) supported it when a mother's life was in danger, and 48.7 percent (including 41.8 percent of regular Mass attendees) favored it after rape had occurred (Rayo and Porath 1990, 37–43).

Ironically, survey data on Chilean Pentecostal opinion (reported earlier) indicate greater support by them for the positions of the bishops than by Catholic laity. Over three-fifths of Chilean Pentecostals (62.9 percent) in 1990 and 1991 were against the legalization of divorce, and more than four-fifths (82.3 percent) were also against the legalization of abortion (Fontaine Talavera and Beyer 1991, 95–96).

Although these surveys are not broken down by class and also do not distinguish among the practicing, between the "sacramentals" (who just attend weekly Mass) and the "organizationals" (who participate in ritual regularly and are also active in the various lay ministries at the local level of the Church), Michael Fleet and I found a considerable basis for potential dissent with the Chilean hierarchy among those in poor areas of Santiago in 1987 who belonged to religious movements or who were involved in base communities or social organizations. Over one-fourth (26.1 percent) of those in religious groups, and over two-fifths (43.6 percent) in CEBs or social projects indicated that they would follow their own consciences rather than the official teachings of the Church if there was a discrepancy between the two. In Lima the figures among comparable groups of low-income Catholic "organizationals" were 35.9 percent in religious groups who supported conscience over authority, and 39.6 percent in CEBs or social organizations who did so (Fleet and B. Smith 1997, 189, 262).

These findings of an emerging trend towards more independent moral thinking among those participating in the new programs at the local level of the Chilean and Peruvian Catholic Churches are corroborated by Daniel Levine in his study of local Catholic activists in Colombia and Venezuela. During in-depth interviews with participants in CEBs and other local Church programs in poor areas of these countries during the 1980s, he found the same inclination to follow one's own conscience over and against the official teachings of the Church when there is a disagreement between the two. He observes that:

> Taken together, the reactions collected . . . reveal a group whose deep involvement with the church is marked by a growing sense of independence from its direction. They remain persons committed to the church but who no longer see themselves as lesser or subordinate individuals. . . .
> . . . Personal independence is also prized and is best expressed in

the ethic of rough egalitarianism that emerges in attitudes towards priests and sisters and to the general question of obedience. (Levine 1992, 311–13)

Hence, both among the small minority in the wealthier sectors of society and among the vast majority who live in modest or very poor conditions, Latin American Catholics—including those who practice regularly and those who are the backbone of the new pastoral programs—exhibit significant differences of opinion from the positions being staunchly defended by the bishops. Not all classes disagree on the same issues, nor have the disagreements reached such a crisis point to date that the bishops are demanding compliance under pain of excommunication. These independent attitudes of laity, however, are an indication that the Catholic Church is seriously divided on some important issues the bishops have made moral priorities in their public policy agenda. The hierarchy thus may not be able to count on sufficient Catholic lay support to sustain its public agenda in the years ahead. This is already evident on economic policy, and it may prove true in the area of personal and family morality if Catholic lay dissent on these issues continues.

The current Catholic Church in Latin America is neither withdrawing from the public arena to concentrate on a purely spiritual agenda, nor has dissent with official Church teachings reached such a proportion as to create the conditions for a schism. Neither does the Church seem to be undergoing a period of readjustment so that it will be able to play a uniformly moderating and consensus-building role on important public moral issues in the near future. The positions staked out by the hierarchy on economic policy and sexual morality are uncompromising and not easily modified by political negotiation and compromise. Nor is there overwhelming support by Catholics of any stripe (culturals, sacramentals, or organizationals) sufficient to implement the public agenda of the hierarchy.

4

FUTURE PENTECOSTAL/CATHOLIC SCENARIOS

In this final chapter I shall assess what the future social and political impact may be resulting from recent changes in Protestantism and Catholicism in Latin America. I shall return to the three possible scenarios articulated in chapter one to determine which is more likely in light of current trends evidenced in the literature.

1. Mutually Reinforcing Flight from the World

I suggested that one possible outcome of the religious changes underway in Latin America would be a declining interest in citizenship responsibilities and participation. Tendencies toward an otherworldly focus in both Pentecostalism and a more conservative Catholicism might act in tandem as mutually reinforcing drawbacks to community involvement in newly constituted democracies. A Pentecostal and Catholic Christianity more focused on issues of personal salvation and private morality could also reduce the number of bishops, priests, nuns, and ministers willing to support social justice for the poor and defend human rights and democratic processes against authoritarian solutions to complex societal problems. Churches thus would become a "refuge from the world," insulating members from the hopes and struggles of their fellow citizens to build more just and participatory societies.

Although this scenario is the logical projection of the analysis of some authors (Lalive d'Epinay, Bastian, Langton, and Mutchler), the evidence in the literature does not support the likelihood that such a scenario will characterize most of Pentecostalism and Catholicism in the coming years.

The primary concerns of Pentecostals thus far do remain in the realms of personal spiritual growth and improvement of family relations. There is also a growing tendency among Catholic bishops and activist laity to emphasize similar concerns so as to offset the socially activist and political role the Catholic Church played during the long years of military rule. It is also true that survey data indicate that, on the whole, the more one is involved in church activities (Pentecostal or Catholic) the less likely one is to join civic or political organizations. There is then some correlation between new religious tendencies underway in Latin America and a focus on more private rather than public concerns.

However, there is also strong evidence that committed Catholics have not retreated from politics, and a growing number of Pentecostals are beginning to show greater interest in public affairs. Catholic bishops throughout Latin America, including many of the newer and more theologically conservative cohort, have spoken out repeatedly about the necessity of social justice for the poor, full disclosure of human rights abuses under previous military regimes, more honesty in government, and laws respecting traditional sexual morality.

While not many Pentecostal pastors have yet staked out public stances on such issues, educational efforts by progressive theologians in mainline Protestant denominations are geared towards making Pentecostal leaders more aware that structural inequities, not merely lapses in personal morality, should be part of their pastoral concern. International meetings organized by the theologically progressive Latin American Theological Fraternity (FTL) and courses in mainline Protestant seminaries for Pentecostal divinity students and pastors are reinforcing the growing importance of a societal focus in Pentecostal morality. Moreover, the vast majority of rank-and-file Pentecostal church members come from low-income sectors of society and the exposure to chronic poverty may very well in time stimulate a more prophetic stance by their pastors against social injustice—as happened to Catholic bishops, priests, and nuns once they began to locate more of their ministries among the urban and rural poor in the 1960s and 1970s.

At the local levels of both denominations—Catholic and Pentecostal—there are also important minorities involved in civic and political organizations. Some of the most articulate and committed leaders of Catholic base communities are also members of local community associations, unions, and political parties in countries such as Brazil, Chile, and Peru. There is also evidence that some Pentecostals are joining civic organizations aimed at improvement of neighborhood services when these do not engage in strong confrontational tactics to achieve their aim and when Pentecostals have a critical mass of followers in a given region.

Although more survey work needs to be done, the evidence so far in Central America (Coleman, Steigenga, Stein, Zub, and Williams) indicates that the vast majority of Pentecostals (70 percent in the early 1990s) do vote. In Guatemala, Peru, and Brazil, presidential candidates have explicitly courted the Pentecostal vote in recent years and in Guatemala (the presidency) and Peru (the second vice presidency) Pentecostals have reached high executive office.

Moreover, there are now Christian political parties founded by Pentecostal lay leaders in seven countries of Latin America who are promoting candidates for office in competitive elections. In Brazil, where four such Christian parties are now functioning, a number of Pentecostals (seventeen) are seated in the congress. Studies of these parties in Brazil and Nicaragua also indicate that their candidates sometimes espouse some similar goals to those of contemporary Catholic leaders—an end to corruption in government, promotion of family values in law, and equitable economic policies for the poor.

All of this evidence indicates that a theologically conservative and spiritually focused Catholicism and Pentecostalism are not moving in tandem to place strong dampers on citizenship. Large numbers of laity are not activists in parties, but they do participate in elections and there is evidence that significant minorities express concerns for public affairs. Should the educational efforts to widen the moral perspectives of Pentecostal pastors be successful in the years ahead, more may come to be as outspoken as Catholic bishops are on critical public policy issues and offer important legitimacy to the parties that some of their activist laity have founded in recent years.

2. Conflicting Religiopolitical Agendas

The second scenario I offered as a possibility at the beginning of this book was that Catholicism and Pentecostalism would each come to espouse very different socioeconomic and political agendas—one of them supportive of free-market economies and democracy, and the other demanding state controls on the economy and political authoritarianism. If such occurred, extremist political factions (on the right and the left respectively) might find moral legitimacy in either denomination for positions antithetical to democratic values and thus manipulate religion for their radical agendas.

A more theologically conservative Catholicism, for example, might result in official episcopal support for corporatist political and economic policies (which the Church flirted with both in Latin America and Europe in the 1930s and 1940s). At the other extreme, those espousing liberation theology at the local level of the Church might join forces with leftist political movements dissatisfied with the progress that newly constituted civilian democracies have made in reducing poverty and agitate for armed revolt. Pentecostalism, in contrast, with its focus on hard work and individual responsibility, would then act as the defender of free-market capitalism and political democracy (as happened historically in England and the United States).

The roles might be reversed, however. The official efforts of Rome to reign in a socially activist Latin American Catholicism might only result in restoring a greater balance and moderation in the Church. The progressive gains made after Vatican II towards a more decentralized, lay-led Church concerned about societal equity and human rights would be consolidated, not jettisoned, and the legitimizing weight of the Church would remain on the side of social justice for the poor within a democratic, capitalist framework. Many Pentecostals, on the other hand, might continue their pattern of tacit, if not open, support for authoritarianism begun when the militaries were in power in Latin America—especially if newly constituted democracies fall prey to corruption and also fail to control mounting social unrest by the poor hurt by current economic restructuring.

Such a dichotomous scenario, or variations of it, seems to be the logical outcome of the analysis offered by some of the strongest critics and the most enthusiastic supporters of contemporary Catholicism and Pentecostalism in Latin America. When all the evidence is weighed together, however, it seems very unlikely that either Catholicism or Pentecostalism will legitimize extremist economic or political movements in the foreseeable future.

Painful memories of both military rule and various socialist experiments in Latin America from the 1960s to the 1980s have made most Catholic bishops wary of authoritarian political policies and statist economic policies. All the major episcopal statements throughout the region in the 1980s and early 1990s in defense of social justice for the poor, honesty in government, and the promotion of family values in law have also been strongly supportive of democratic policy-making among party leaders to achieve these objectives. The fact that Catholic bishops have been asked since the early 1980s to serve as mediators between government and armed opposition forces to achieve an end to civil war in several Central American countries and in Mexico, Colombia, and Peru has underscored this commitment of the official Church to civil peace within a democratic framework.

Moreover, all the extant survey research on attitudes of local Catholic activists throughout the continent have shown that both the leaders and members of Catholic-sponsored religious and social programs reflect attitudes that are compatible with both capitalism and democracy (a propensity for hard work, savings, a sober lifestyle, and toleration and compromise in politics). Moreover, these local Catholic communities seem to be enhancing the capacities and willingness of their adherents to think for themselves and to improve their personal and family lives. Even if the majority do not become activists in civic or political organizations, their values are not antithetical to democratic processes in society.

The more radical attitudes and behavior associated with those espousing liberation theology in the 1960s and early 1970s do not seem to be characteristic of the vast majority of Catholic activists in Latin America today. There are party differences (from right to left) among practicing Catholics, and class does make a significant difference in political preference. The parties supported by Catholic laity closely involved in the life of the Church, however, are supportive of constitutionalism and of peaceful ways of resolving societal problems.

On the Pentecostal side, there is no current evidence pointing to public endorsement of authoritarian rule. It is true that some Pentecostals openly, or tacitly, gave support to repressive military regimes in Central America and the Southern Cone region in the 1970s and 1980s due to the avowed anti-Marxist objectives of these governments. Now, however, in these countries as well as elsewhere in Latin America, Pentecostals are fairly comfortable with newly constituted democracies, and in no case has there been a public espousal by Pentecostal leaders for a return to authoritarian rule. The fact that there are new Christian political parties founded primarily as a result of Pentecostal initiatives which now compete in electoral politics is an indication that those laity who do engage in politics are committed to do so within a democratic framework.

Moreover, despite internal control of Pentecostal communities by pastors who demand strict obedience to their directives, the attitudes of rank-and-file members display many of the same patterns that characterize Catholic lay activists—a growing sense of their own self-worth, more discipline in personal and family life, a propensity towards hard work and savings, a repugnance for human rights violations, and a desire for social justice for the poor. Even though to date the vast majority of Pentecostals are not involved in civic or political organizations, their attitudes and behavior are more supportive of democratic than authoritarian values in civic culture.

It is also true that within Catholicism, and beginning in Pentecostalism as well, there are sharp criticisms of an unbridled capitalism that operates only for the sake of profit with no social conscience. Catholic bishops throughout the region, following the pope's lead, have repeatedly criticized severe government cutbacks in social services that have increased hardships on the poor. They have also condemned drastic reductions in tariffs that have caused many local businesses to fail, thus exacerbating unemployment. Pentecostal ministers have yet to be as sharply and consistently outspoken in their criticisms of the dominant economic model throughout Latin America, but the joint statements issued at international conferences organized for Pentecostal pastors by FTL, the voting records of Pentecostal deputies and senators in national congresses, and the official policies of several of the new political parties founded by Pentecostals all indicate their growing uneasiness with the dismantling of many public services and controls over trade and investments that are hurting the poor throughout the region.

Neither Catholicism nor Pentecostalism seems to have significant numbers within their respective ranks espousing either political authoritarianism or radicalism. Nor is there a call from either camp for economic statism or unbridled free-market competition. Thus, in both camps there is evidence emerging that moderate economic and political views characterize the vast majority of leaders and followers alike. It is unlikely that in the foreseeable future either denomination will be a breeding ground for attitudes or behavior antithetical to constitutionalism or capitalism, but both will be uneasy with economic policies that do not begin to improve the quality of life for the poor.

3. Prophetic Social Catalysts Moving in Tandem

The third possibility for these two religious movements is that their overlapping social and religious concerns will bring them closer together in the years ahead in active collaboration and that this will also strengthen the underpinnings of democratic regimes. Given the parallel concerns shared by both, and the similar moral values they are inculcating among their respective laity, they very well may become collaborators in combining their respective social services for the poor, in jointly speaking out on behalf of more equitable public policies, and in serving as training grounds for a new generation of civic-minded adults ready to offer their opinions and services to the wider secular community.

There certainly is clear evidence that these two denominations are coming to resemble one another on many fronts—serious commitment to work among the poor, pastoral emphasis on Bible study and prayer, greater use of the media to spread the gospel message, strengthening lay involvements in congregational associations, building self-esteem and more personal responsibility to family among lay members, growing concern about moral issues affecting society (chronic poverty, alcoholism, abuse of women, and corruption in public office).

One might expect that, given these similarities of goals, styles, and concerns, Catholics and Pentecostals would begin to forge working relationships for mutual learning and sharing and for attacking more effectively the underlying causes of moral problems they decry in the larger society. If it is true that the local communities promoted by Catholics and Pentecostals are now the most vital cultural movements among the poor today in Latin America (as Bryan Froehle and Phillip Berryman have argued), then a collaborative reinforcement of their efforts could only enhance their contribution to strengthening the kind of associational life that underpins stable democracy.

Although there may be some tactical collaboration in the years ahead in trying to influence specific public policy issues, the perennial animosity separating these two denominations will take considerable time to heal. Some of the statements leaders on both sides are making about one another and the serious disagreements they have over the legal privileges of the Catholic Church throughout Latin America make it quite unlikely that any kind of strategic collaboration will occur in the foreseeable future. In fact, in the areas of public policy where they are most likely to join forces to influence law—divorce, abortion, rights of homosexuals, education to prevent the spread of AIDS—their collaboration might very well complicate, rather than enhance, the type of compromise democratic policy-making in pluralistic societies requires.

The long history of strained relations between Catholics and Pentecostals in Latin America has not been forgotten on either side. Even before Pentecostalism began to grow at significant rates in the 1960s, Catholic bishops and priests were openly critical of Pentecostals as being foreign agents subverting the traditional cultural ties of Latin Americans to Catholicism. Although Pentecostals have come to depend less on foreign personnel and money and now are clearly an indigenous movement, official Catholic accusations of their being a foreign subversive force have continued. Pope John Paul II's reference to them in Santo Domingo in 1992 as "rapacious wolves" funded from abroad and devouring Catholic souls was most offensive. The sweeping generalization made by some contemporary Latin American bishops that Pentecostals are paid agents of the CIA only adds fuel to a fire of resentment that has been simmering for decades.

Despite the growing concern among Catholic leaders about the dramatic growth of Pentecostalism and its success in luring cultural and lapsed Catholics into its ranks, Catholics have made little effort to engage these fellow Christians in dialogue or to get to know them on a personal level. Phillip Berryman found in his studies of Catholic and Pentecostal communities in São Paulo, Brazil, and Caracas, Venezuela, in 1993, that in a few short months in each city he was better informed about the beliefs and practices of Pentecostals and had more personal contact with them than Catholic clerical and lay leaders he interviewed who live in these cities. Catholic concern about Pentecostalism has not led to engagement of their world; rather, it has often stimulated a form of stereotyping and name-calling of Pentecostalism that has produced a "holy war" mindset (Berryman 1996, 185, 191).

Conversely, some Pentecostal pastors still view the Church of Rome as the Antichrist and warn their congregations against any form of contact with Catholics. On the eve of Pope John Paul II's visit to La Paz, Bolivia, in 1987, a Pentecostal preacher railed against idolatry among Catholics who, he claimed, worship pieces of wood and who falsely rely on intermediaries between themselves and God. The pastor also charged that Satan runs rampant through convents and monasteries spreading fornication, homosexuality, and secret abortions by nuns (L. Gill 1993, 188).

A survey during the late 1980s and early 1990s in Mexico indicated that 54 percent of Pentecostal pastors did not believe that Catholics were true Christians nor part of the body of Christ. Their core reasons were that Catholics "practice idolatry" by "worshipping images" and that Catholics lack a "personal relationship with Jesus Christ" (Bowen 1996, 127–28). A survey of Pentecostal pastors in Chile in the early 1990s revealed that, despite a growing exposure to mainstream Protestant theology through some seminary training, 61 percent rejected the idea of dialogue with Catholics (Gilfeather 1992, 64).

In October 1995 a Brazilian Pentecostal pastor of the Universal Church of the Reign of God, the fastest growing church in Brazil, on a televised religious program destroyed a statue of Brazil's patron saint, Our Lady of Aparecida, claiming it was a form of idolatry for Catholics. Both the Catholic bishops and Globo TV, the fourth largest television network in the world which is owned by a conservative Catholic layman, claimed that such a tactic was a threat to freedom of religion in Brazil. The pastor was forced to resign (Tautz 1995). The controversy raged for months, and government officials began to investigate financial dealings of the Universal Church in the aftermath of the incident (Berryman 1996, 191; Serbin 1997, 11; Tautz 1997). Such abusive public words and actions on both sides against the other are not conducive to mutual understanding nor to the development of collaboration.

More serious obstacles to collaboration have been the disagreements over the long tradition in most Latin American countries of Catholic privileges in law and the recent demands by Catholic bishops that governments put legal restrictions on Pentecostal churches. One of the goals of the new political parties founded by Pentecostals in Brazil and in Nicaragua has been to remove special mention of Catholicism in the respective national constitutions and to end public subsidies to Catholic schools. Similar efforts by Pentecostal pastors to end Catholic privileges are underway in Argentina, Ecuador, Bolivia, and Paraguay. Catholic bishops in these countries have strongly denounced efforts to restrict the Catholic Church's legal privileges, and they have used personal contacts with public officials to block legislation promoting such initiatives. In some countries (Argentina and Chile) they have also insisted that governments impose registration requirements on every new non-Catholic church that is formed.

Hence, there is more at stake than acrimonious words and hard feelings between Catholics and Pentecostals. The issue of full separation of church and state now that religious pluralism is growing in Latin America is becoming an important political debate. If this legislative initiative, supported by many Pentecostals, is successful the Catholic Church would lose public moneys for its significant educational network throughout Latin America and would be treated as any other denomination by the law. If the current privileges for Catholicism are maintained, however, and, in addition, new restrictions are placed on other denominations, Pentecostals as they grow will have to accept a subservient role in law and continue to have some of their laity's tax money go towards supporting a different church.

Until this thorny constitutional issue of unequal treatment of denominations before the law is settled, there is little hope of any strategic alliance between Catholics and Pentecostals. In fact, there is growing evidence that each side sees the demands of the other as morally unacceptable and politically nonnegotiable. Tensions are also spilling over into the public realm since legislators are feeling pressures either to keep the constitution and the laws the way they are or to remove all mention and support for Catholicism in public documents. This issue of complete separation of church and state could become a divisive element in party politics in the years ahead, especially if both denominations continue to push their respective causes so adamantly.

Although such tensions and political disagreements while they last will seriously reduce the chances of collaboration, there are some signs of limited collaboration, especially at the local level. In the state of Chiapas, Mexico, Pentecostals have been persecuted by merchants for over two decades for not participating in Catholic festivals honoring the saints. Landowners have seized their properties and shopkeepers have hounded them from their homes in San Juan Chamula and several other villages in the mountains near San Cristóbal de las Casas, the capital. The reason is that Pentecostals (most of whom are former Catholics) do not purchase candles, statues, and liquor that have become ingredients in these Catholic celebrations, thus cutting into the profits of the local elites. The Catholic bishop of San Cristóbal, Samuel Ruiz, set up a special program, "Serving Our Peoples" (SYJAC), to assist these persecuted Pentecostals. SYJAC provides economic and educational services to Pentecostals expelled from their villages and has helped coordinate a home rebuilding program for Pentecostals whose houses have been destroyed (Jeffrey 1996b). In Argentina, there are also instances at the local level where Catholic and Pentecostal congregations have collaborated in providing services to the jobless as unemployment continues to rise, up to 17.1 percent in 1996–97 (Plou 1996).

There also may emerge a growing reinforcement for one another's stance on issues of family values and sexual morality in law. There are moves being made in several Latin American countries to expand the conditions for legal abortions, to legalize divorce or liberalize the conditions for it, to grant legal protection for the rights of homosexuals, and to mount AIDS education campaigns in government media encouraging the use of condoms in casual sexual relations. Catholic bishops have been adamant and persistent in their opposition to all of these initiatives and so also have leaders of newly formed political parties associated with Pentecostalism.

There have been some instances where tacit, or even open, collaboration by Catholics and Pentecostals has occurred to pursue a common objective in the area of sexual morality. In 1995 in Chile both the Catholic bishops and leaders of several Pentecostal churches at about the same time denounced proposed changes in law that would grant equal rights to homosexuals ("Chile: No Homosexuals Please" 1995). In Costa Rica in 1993, after separately opposing a proposed sex education program for public schools that would condone the use of safe sex outside of marriage, Catholic bishops and Pentecostal pastors developed a sex education program together that encouraged abstinence from sexual relations outside of marriage as the best way to stop sexually transmitted diseases ("Costa Rica" 1993).

While these are isolated cases they may also be indications of the start of a tactical alliance between the two denominations where they have identical and deeply felt concerns about the treatment of sexual morality in law. If these cases are multiplied and lead to jointly planned campaigns, they could have a significant impact on policy-making. At the very least, they could slow down the process of change in these areas that are now being seriously considered by lawmakers and pushed by various women's organizations and civil rights advocates as necessary for public health and for respecting individual sexual preferences.

On one hand, every group in a democratic society—including churches—is entitled to pressure policymakers for laws it believes are right for the common good. On the other hand, liberal democracy is also predicated on majority rule. Minority rights are to be respected, but minorities are not to impose their views on the majority when it is clear that they are minority views. In the cases of divorce, abortion, civil rights for those choosing alternative lifestyles, and the need for effective public education to stop the spread of deadly diseases, public opinion polls in various Latin American countries indicate that significant majorities are in favor of changes.

Catholic and Pentecostal leaders may oppose divorce, abortion, homosexuality, and safe sex outside marriage on moral grounds and urge their respective laity not to engage in such practices in their personal lives. They also have the right to educate the wider public about what they believe to be the moral dangers of such practices for society as a whole and try, through the pulpit and the media, to mold public opinion in favor of their church's position. But if the majority of citizens in a democratic society, after hearing the voice of churches on moral issues, does not accept these positions, clerical resort to political pressure to impose church views in law complicates the democratic process. Churches do have moral influence that other pressure groups do not have, especially in a traditionally Christian culture such as Latin America. Using this resource to impose on all of society a clearly minority opinion on a complex moral issue tends to erode the credibility of churches as promoters of democracy. It interjects into a political process requiring negotiation for its success an inflexible approach to solving public problems that is antithetical to liberal democracy.

From the perspectives of Catholic and Pentecostal leaders, important moral issues are not subject to the same kind of give-and-take as are political and economic issues—particularly if they are understood as being God's universal law for all people. In such instances, clerics would fail in their pastoral responsibility if they did not use every legal means to stop what they see to be direct countermands to this universal moral law in society. Some forms of the Christian religion and liberal democracy, therefore, are not always comfortable partners since churches cannot be counted on to support majority rule in all situations. Conservative Christianity (reflected in official Catholicism and Pentecostalism) and democratic policy-making are premised on two different conceptions of truth (one absolute, the other relative) and how to achieve it (one through obedience to divine command, and the other through human compromise).[1]

Two policy areas where Catholic/Pentecostal interaction is occurring in the public forum at present—church/state separation, and sexual morality in law—complicate, not support, the process of democratic politics. On both issues, absolutist positions have been staked out by Catholic and Pentecostal leaders in which negotiation has thus far been ruled out. Such strongly held moral views by leaders of large denominations will complicate policy-making in the years ahead and may precipitate bitter religiopolitical battles—in some cases pitting Catholic bishops against Pentecostal pastors, and in others placing them on the same side in opposing the will of the majority of their fellow citizens.

What may dampen the effect of such disputes in the public arena is the fact that large numbers of Catholic laity do not support the positions of the hierarchy on some of these complex moral issues. There is evidence of disagreement within the Catholic Church between practicing Catholics and bishops over the desirability of legalized divorce and abortion, and local Catholic activists engaged in the ritual or organizational life of the Church also demonstrate a high degree of tolerance for the rights of minorities in society. If the hierarchy attempts to mount a major public effort to stop legal reforms on such issues as divorce, abortion, rights of homosexuals, and equal treatment of all churches in law, opposition may emerge from some of the very cadres the bishops count on to back up their positions. In the very least, there are not likely to be large numbers of Catholic laity willing to engage in public demonstrations or to lobby legislators in support of the official Church's position on several of these episcopal priorities. Under such circumstances, policymakers would be able to ignore the hierarchy's demands at less political cost since many Catholic laity would not penalize them at the ballot box.

Attitudinal surveys of Pentecostals indicate that laity in those denominations are much closer to their official churches' positions on divorce and abortion and more intolerant in accepting minority rights in society than are most Catholic laity. Pentecostal pastors may have more unified congregations willing to back them up if they, or the new political parties formed by Pentecostals, decide to mount major public campaigns to stop legal changes favoring divorce, abortion, equal rights for homosexuals, media education supporting safe sex outside marriage, and removal of Catholic privileges in law.

However, there are other indications that may weaken the political impact of Pentecostals on policy-making in the years ahead. There is evidence that the rapid growth of Pentecostalism may be peaking in some regions (Altmann 1996). Studies in Guatemala (Evans 1990), El Salvador (Confraternidad Evangélica Salvadoreña [CONESAL] 1987), Costa Rica (Kessler 1992), and Mexico (Bowen 1996) all point to a declining rate of growth of Pentecostal churches. A 1989 study conducted in Costa Rica, for example, indicated that although 8.9 percent identified themselves as Pentecostal, another 8.1 percent said they no longer were. Of these, 62 percent had returned to the Catholic Church and 31 percent no longer professed any religion. In a repeat survey in 1991 the percentage of Pentecostals who had left their new denominations rose to 12.1 percent. In Mexico recidivism now has reached 48 percent among second-generation converts (Kessler 1992; Jeffrey 1996a, 6; Bowen 1996, 71; Hallum 1996, 61–62).

The reasons offered by those studying this new development include dissatisfaction with the inability of women to become full pastors, the poor quality of preaching and teaching by uneducated ministers, clerical mishandling of funds, "burnout" from efforts to live up to the rigorous moral demands of Pentecostalism, the attractions of materialism among better-off converts, and uneasiness with a life of isolation from one's non-Pentecostal neighbors. "Poaching" of members by other Pentecostal churches looking to expand and the new aggressive evangelization campaigns by Catholics have also been identified as reasons for stalled Pentecostal growth.

If the growth rate of Pentecostal churches is peaking, even if pastors and Pentecostal-inspired parties become more vocal on public moral issues, their political weight will not be as significant as some projections have assumed. Pastors simply will not have sufficient numbers of laity to block legal changes in sexual morality that the majority of citizens want. This limitation, coupled with only a minority of Catholics backing up their bishops on the same issues, will reduce significantly the influence both denominations will have in stopping these changes.

The future of Catholicism and Pentecostalism appears complex. Sharply defined scenarios for both denominations are inadequate, and they are likely to remain so in the foreseeable future. Neither church will retreat totally from politics, nor will either attempt to subvert constitutional government. They both have potentially important contributions for the strengthening of democratic rule. Despite many shared concerns, it is also unlikely that there will emerge a broad Pentecostal/Catholic alliance in the near future. Ironically, despite their positive contributions to democracy, on some issues in which cooperation in politics may emerge, the result might also complicate, rather than bolster, consensus-building in Latin American society.

NOTES

1 Pentecostal Expansion, Catholic Retrenchment

1. Pentecostalism resembles on several points Evangelical Christianity more than it does the historic Protestant traditions associated with the Reformation (Lutheranism, Calvinism, Anglicanism). Like Evangelicals, Pentecostals emphasize the inerrancy of Scripture, the centrality of Bible over sacrament in worship, the decentralized nature of the church, and the responsibility of each member to spread the faith. Pentecostals place much more emphasis, however, on identifying visible signs of the Holy Spirit in one's life, such as praying in tongues, emotional or physical healings, and exorcisms. They also emphasize much less than Evangelicals the importance of scholarship in understanding the meaning of Scripture. Evangelical Christians are also growing in number in Latin America but nowhere near the rate of Pentecostals, and not as much among the lower classes as are Pentecostals.

2. American sociologist Christian Smith and American political scientist Michael Dodson have each emphasized similar optimism about the potential contributions of Pentecostalism to the future of Latin American democracy (C. Smith 1995, 18–21; Dodson 1997, 31–37). Some U.S. journalists, writing for business-oriented magazines, have also picked up on the positive assessments of Willems and Martin and predict that Pentecostalism may give free enterprise the moral boost it needs to solve Latin America's chronic problems of poverty (Ryser et al. 1990; Marcom 1990).

3. Differences exist among Latin American liberation theologians as to the extent of official political involvements by clergy and the legitimacy of the use of violence to achieve change. For a representative sample of these various positions, see Hennelly, 1990.

4. This scenario resonates with the analysis of scholars a generation ago for whom the Church was perennially a conservative institution whose preferred allies are always those groups defending the established order in society— large landholders, industrial and commercial elites, financiers, and the military. For Mutchler (1971), Langton (1976, 1986), Grigulevich (1984), and Gismondi (1986), the reforms in the 1960s and 1970s were tactically defensive moves to improve the Church's chances of surviving working-class ascendancy in politics, democratic forms of socialism, Marxist revolutions, and military authoritarianism. The implication of their position was that reforms in the Church to meet such challenges were merely cosmetic, did not penetrate the power structure of the institution, and would be reversed once all these social crises in society had passed (as they now have). For a recent articulation of this position, in somewhat modified form, see Daudelin and Hewitt, 1995.

5. This scenario finds plausibility in the analysis of some research in the 1980s and early 1990s that concluded that the Church was seriously polarized between

higher and lower levels (Lernoux 1989; Crahan 1982, 1984; Sigmund 1990) or that its growing lower-class adherents in base communities were creating a new Church different from the one that still characterized wealthier Catholics (Berryman 1984; Foroohar 1989). Some of these scholars in their more recent research have ruled out the likelihood of schism in the Church, observing that its basic institutional unity is in tact despite "sharp theological, political and ideological divisions" (Crahan 1991, 153; Berryman 1994a, 1996).

6. This scenario is the likely outcome implicit in the work of Levine (1981, 1992), Bruneau (1974, 1982), B. Smith (1982), Mainwaring (1986), and Winn (1992), all of whom are optimistic about the continued moderating role of the Church in social reform in the years ahead despite some internal readjustments underway.

7. Over the past century, Catholicism has officially voiced serious reservations about the capitalist system. All papal encyclicals that have dealt with socioeconomic problems since the 1890s, and all major pastoral letters of the Latin American bishops on economic issues since the 1960s, have accepted capitalism only under the condition that vigorous state action be taken to offer ample public services for the poor and impose legal controls on the free market system to ensure that private property serves the common good (Walsh and Davies 1991; Latin American Episcopal Conference (CELAM) 1970, 1979; Cleary 1989; Hennelly 1993).

8. Since Aristotle, many political theorists have argued that the health of representative government depends upon economic conditions that diminish economic differences among social groups and open up opportunities for an expanding middle class (Aristotle 1984; Hartz 1955; Lipset 1960).

2 Explanations and Implications of Pentecostal Growth

1. For an excellent review of some of the previous seminars, consultations, and meetings that predated the 1989 Buenos Aires and 1992 Quito conferences and which involved Latin American Pentecostals discussing the relationship between evangelism and social responsibility, see Nuñez and Taylor, 1989, 367–405.

2. In Brazil, the Brazilian Evangelical Association (AEVB), a federation of Protestant churches founded in 1991, has also attempted to promote more dialogue and respect among mainline and Pentecostal churches. In the process it has helped to stimulate a greater commitment to social justice among the Pentecostals (Freston 1993, 106; Cook 1994b, 137–38).

3 Assessment of Contemporary Catholicism

1. Two countries where episcopal public support for a return to democracy has not been particularly strong in the 1990s are Haiti and Cuba. When democratically elected president Rev. Jean-Bertrand Aristide was overthrown by the Haitian military in September 1991 the hierarchy did not criticize the move. Aristide, an ordained cleric, contravened the Vatican policy of forbidding priests from holding public office. The Vatican was also one of the few governments to recognize that military junta during its two years in power, and neither the pope

nor the Haitian bishops supported the subsequent U.S. government intervention to restore Aristide to the presidency (Greene 1993, 246–47; Rohter 1994a and b). In Cuba, neither the bishops nor the Vatican have been strong public supporters of a return to democracy, but rather have dialogued privately in recent years with the Castro regime to gain various concessions for the Church. They have negotiated successfully for greater contacts with the international Church, for permission for foreign priests and nuns once again to work in Cuba, and for removal of restrictions forbidding religious believers from being members of the Communist Party. Although international Church representatives have been successful in obtaining the release of some Cuban political prisoners, gaining more religious freedoms has taken priority over Church defense of other civil and political liberties in Cuba (Treaster 1988a and b, 1989; Kirk 1989, pp. 169–78; Domínguez 1989; Chauvin 1996). During his January 1998 visit to Cuba, the pope did publicly underscore the importance of other civil liberties, such as freedom of expression and association but placed greatest emphasis on "the exercise of the freedom of conscience—the basis and foundation of all other human rights" (Rohter 1998).

2. In late April 1998 the release of a 1,400-page report by the Truth Commission, "Guatemala: Never Again!" met with violent reaction. Based on almost 7,000 interviews over a three-year period, it accused the Guatemalan military and paramilitary squads associated with them for more than 80 percent of the 150,000 deaths and 50,000 disappearances during the long civil war that ended in 1996. Bishop Juan Gerardi, the episcopal coordinator of the study, was assassinated two days later by an unknown assailant. A right-wing paramilitary group publicly claimed responsibility for the murder, but as this book went to press (July 1998) there was to date no information released by the government as to who was responsible for the crime. The Catholic bishops have criticized the government for what they consider to be a lack of political will to uncover the facts and bring the perpetrators to justice.

3. In Argentina, divorce was also illegal until the civilian administration of Raúl Alfonsín, in the wake of the 1983 military withdrawal from executive power, proposed to Congress a legislative package aimed at consolidating democracy. Part of the reforms included the legalization of divorce. The bishops strongly opposed the legislation, but failed in their efforts to block it. Its subsequent passage by the legislature in 1986 seriously strained relations between the Catholic Church and the democratic government (M. Burdick 1995, 240–46).

4. It is difficult to assess the full monetary value of all of the material and financial assistance that these international Catholic agencies provide to the Latin American Catholic Church each year. There is no central Church office, even in Rome, that tracks all of this aid. It is administered by national Church agencies in Europe, Canada, and the United States which operate independently of one another and which deal on a project-by-project basis with groups in Latin America. Moreover, all of these Catholic funding agencies also support non-Church-sponsored projects in Latin America if they are tailored to meet effectively some social need of the poor. Many of these groups, however, if not—or no longer—Church-sponsored normally maintain working relationships with Church personnel or include Catholic lay persons with close ties to the local nun or priest who has often facilitated their access to foreign Catholic

funding agencies. Despite these data limitations, some approximations can be made. About $10 billion annually from North Atlantic nonprofit service agencies (secular and religious) now flows to private groups to aid the poor in the third world. About one-third of these funds go to Latin America ($3 billion), and 60 percent are channeled through Catholic and Protestant service agencies ($1.8 billion). The Catholic agencies tend to be larger than their Protestant counterparts, so a very rough estimation of the amount coming through international Catholic organizations for Latin American social service and development projects annually is probably now in the vicinity of $1 billion (B. Smith 1998).

5. In my own pastoral work as a priest in 1975 in a shantytown in Santiago, Chile, I found this same split between the "pray-ers" and the "do-ers." Those involved in the neocatechumenate wanted only to pray and discuss personal spiritual issues among themselves, and they seldom would offer their time to ministries concerned with feeding the hungry, helping the unemployed, or assisting those whose rights were being chronically violated by the military regime.

6. In fact, some scholars have already documented the shrinkage of Brazilian CEB membership precisely because those most interested in working for social justice or who are the most "politically astute" have exited base communities. They find secular organizations more attractive and effective in pursuing their objectives (Mainwaring 1989, 173).

4 Future Pentecostal/Catholic Scenarios

1. Not all denominations within Christianity take such absolutist positions on moral issues as reflected in public law as do Catholicism and Pentecostalism. For a discussion of alternate religious viewpoints (especially within Christianity) on how to relate moral principles to policy-making in a democratic society, see Thiemann, 1996.

REFERENCES

Adriance, Madeleine. 1986. *Opting for the Poor: Brazilian Catholicism in Transition.* Kansas City: Sheed and Ward.

——. 1995. "Base Communities and Rural Mobilization in Northern Brazil." In *Religion and Democracy in Latin America,* ed. Swatos, pp. 59–74.

ALC. 1997. "Bolivia: Evangelicals Joining Political Fray." *Latinamerica Press* (Lima) 29, no. 19 (May 22): 6.

Altmann, Rev. Walter. 1996. "Religious Pluralism in Latin America." *Latinamerica Press* 28, no. 42 (November 14): 3.

Alvarez Gandara, Miguel. 1992. "Santo Domingo: Doloroso avance de la iglesia de América Latina." *CHRISTUS* (Mexico City) 58, nos. 660/61 (November/December): 50–71.

Alves, Rubem. 1985. *Protestantism and Repression: A Brazilian Case Study.* Maryknoll, N.Y.: Orbis.

Annis, Sheldon. 1987. *God and Production in a Guatemalan Town.* Austin, Tex.: University of Texas Press.

Aristotle. 1984. *The Politics.* Trans. by Carnes Lord. Chicago: University of Chicago Press.

Arroyo, Victor, and Tito Paredes. 1992. "Evangelicals and 'The Fujimori Phenomenon.' " *Transformation* (Exeter, U.K.) 9, no. 3: 15–19.

Assman, Hugo. 1976. *Theology for a Nomad Church.* Maryknoll, N.Y.: Orbis.

——. 1987. *La iglesia electrónica y su impacto en América Latina.* San José, Costa Rica: Departamento Ecuménico de Investigaciones (DEI).

Aubry, Roger. 1990. *La misión siguiendo a Jesús por los caminos de América Latina.* Buenos Aires: Editorial Guadalupe.

Bastian, Jean-Pierre. 1985. "Dissidence religieuse protestante dans le milieu rural Mexicain." *Social Compass* (Brussels) 32, nos. 2/3: 245–60.

——. 1986. "Protestantismo popular y política en Guatemala y Nicaragua." *Revista Mexicana de Sociología* 48, no. 3: 181–200.

——. 1990. *Historia del protestantismo en América Latina.* Mexico City: Casa Unida de Publicaciones.

——. 1992. "Protestantism in Latin America." In *The Church in Latin America: 1492–1992,* ed. Dussel, pp. 313–51.

——. 1993. "The Metamorphosis of Latin American Protestant

Groups: A Sociohistorical Perspective." *Latin American Research Review* 28, no. 2: 33–61.

———. 1997. "Minorités religieuses et confessionnalisation de la politique en Amérique Latine." *Archives des Sciences Sociales des Religions* (Paris), no. 97 (January-March): 97–114.

Bautz, Wolfgang, Noel González, and Javier Orozco. 1994. *Política y religión, estudio de caso: Los evangélicos en Nicaragua.* Managua: Editorial CIEETS and Fundación Friedrich Ebert.

Berg, Clayton L., and Paul E. Pretiz. 1996a. *Spontaneous Combustion: Grassroots Christianity, Latin American Style.* Pasadena, Calif.: William Carey Library.

———. 1996b. "Latin America's Fifth Wave of Protestant Churches." *International Bulletin of Missionary Research* 20, no. 4 (October): 157–59.

Berryman, Phillip. 1984. *The Religious Roots of Rebellion: Christians in Central American Revolutions.* Maryknoll, N.Y.: Orbis.

———. 1994a. *Stubborn Hope: Religion, Politics, and Revolution in Central America.* Maryknoll, N.Y.: Orbis.

———. 1994b. "The Coming of Age of Evangelical Protestantism." *NACLA Report on the Americas* 27, no. 6 (May/June). Reprinted in *LADOC* (Lima) 25 (November/December 1994): 21–27.

———. 1996. *Religion in the Megacity: Catholic and Protestant Portraits from Latin America.* Maryknoll, N.Y.: Orbis.

Blixen, Samuel. 1994. "Social Situation Worries Uruguayan Bishops." *Latinamerica Press* (Lima) 26, no. 18 (May 19): 3.

Boff, Leonardo. 1978. *Jesus Christ Liberator: A Critical Christology for Our Time.* Maryknoll, N.Y.: Orbis.

Boudewijnse, Barbara, André Droogers, and Frans Kamsteeg, eds. 1991. *Algo más que opio: Una lectura anthropológica del pentecostalismo Latinoamericano y Caribeño.* San José, Costa Rica: Editorial Departamento Ecuménico de Investigaciones (DEI).

Bowen, Kurt. 1996. *Evangelism and Apostasy: The Evolution and Impact of Evangelicals in Modern Mexico.* Montreal: McGill-Queen's University Press.

Brooke, James. 1993. "AIDS in Latin America: In Deception and Denial, an Epidemic Looms." *New York Times,* January 25, pp. A1, A5.

———. 1994. "With Church Preaching in Vain, Brazilians Embrace Birth Control." *New York Times,* September 2, pp. A1, A3.

Brouwer, Steve, Paul Gifford, and Susan D. Rose. 1996. *Exporting the American Gospel: Global Christian Fundamentalism.* New York, N.Y.: Routledge.

Bruneau, Thomas C. 1974. *The Political Transformation of the Brazilian Catholic Church.* Cambridge: Cambridge University Press.

———. 1982. *The Church in Brazil: The Politics of Religion.* Austin, Tex.: University of Texas Press.

Bruneau, Thomas C., and W. E. Hewitt. 1992. "Catholicism and Political Action in Brazil: Limitations and Prospects." In *Conflict and Competition: The Latin American Church in a Changing Environment,* ed. Cleary and Stewart-Gambino, pp. 45–62.

Brusco, Elizabeth E. 1993. "The Reformation of Machismo: Asceticism and Masculinity among Colombian Evangelicals." In *Rethinking Protestantism in Latin America,* ed. Garrard-Burnett and Stoll, pp. 143–58.

———. 1995. *The Reformation of Machismo: Evangelical Conversion and Gender in Colombia.* Austin, Tex.: University of Texas Press.

Burdick, John. 1993a. *Looking for God in Brazil.* Berkeley, Calif.: University of California Press.

———. 1993b. "Struggling against the Devil: Pentecostalism and Social Movements in Urban Brazil." In *Rethinking Protestantism in Latin America,* ed. Garrard-Burnett and Stoll, pp. 20–44.

Burdick, Michael A. 1995. *For God and the Fatherland: Religion and Politics in Argentina.* Albany, N.Y.: State University of New York Press.

Cabieses, Javier. 1994. "Divorce Law Proposed in Chile." *Latinamerica Press* 26 (July 14): 3.

Camp, Roderic Ai. 1997. *Crossing Swords: Politics and Religion in Mexico.* New York: Oxford University Press.

Campodonico, Humberto. 1993. "Neoliberalism and Poverty in Latin America." *Latinamerica Press* 25, no. 47 (December 23): 6.

Chauvin, Lucien O. 1995. "Poverty Haunts Latin America's 'Boom.' " *Latinamerica Press* 27, no. 28 (July 27): 1, 8.

———. 1996. "Thaw in Church-State Relations." *Latinamerica Press* 28, no. 44 (November 28): 1, 8.

———. 1997a. "Bishop Plays Key Role in Crisis." *Latinamerica Press* 29, no. 1 (January 16): 4–5.

———. 1997b. "Bishop Helped Gain Soldiers' Release." *Latinamerica Press* 29, no. 24 (June 26): 1, 8.

"Chile." 1990. *Latinamerica Press* 22, no. 47 (December 20): 2.

"Chile: No Homosexuals, Please." 1995. *Latinamerica Press* 27, no. 21 (June 8): 8.

Cleary, Edward L., O.P. 1989. *Path from Puebla: Significant Documents of the Latin American Bishops since 1979.* Washington, D.C.: U.S. Catholic Conference.

———. 1992a. "Evangelicals and Competition in Guatemala." In *Conflict and Competition,* ed. Cleary and Stewart-Gambino, pp. 167–95.

———. 1992b. "Conclusions: Politics and Religion—Crisis, Constraints, and Restructuring." In *Conflict and Competition,* ed. Cleary and Stewart-Gambino, pp. 197–221.

———. 1992c. "John Paul Cries 'Wolf': Misreading the Pentecostals." *Commonweal* (November 20): 7–8.

——. 1994. "Protestants and Catholics: Rivals or Siblings?" In *Coming of Age*, ed. Daniel Miller, pp. 205–27.

——. 1997a. "Introduction: Pentecostals, Prominence, and Politics." In *Power, Politics and Pentecostals in Latin America*, ed. Cleary and Stewart-Gambino, pp. 1–24.

——. 1997b. "The Spirit Moves: Why Pentecostals Thrive in Latin America." *Commonweal* (January 17): 9–10.

Cleary, Edward L., O.P., and Juan Sepúlveda, 1997. "Chilean Pentecostalism: Coming of Age." In *Power, Politics, and Pentecostals in Latin America*, ed. Cleary and Stewart-Gambino, pp. 97–121.

Cleary, Edward L., O.P., and Hannah Stewart-Gambino, eds. 1992. *Conflict and Competition: The Latin American Church in a Changing Environment*. Boulder, Colo.: Lynne Rienner.

——. 1997. *Power, Politics and Pentecostals in Latin America*. Boulder, Colo.: Westview Press.

Colby, Gerard, and Charlotte Dennett. 1995. *Thy Will Be Done: The Conquest of the Amazon — Nelson Rockefeller and Evangelism in the Age of Oil*. New York: HarperCollins.

Coleman, Kenneth M., et al. 1993. "Protestantism in El Salvador: Conventional Wisdom versus the Survey Evidence." In *Rethinking Protestantism in Latin America*, ed. Garrard-Burnett and Stoll, pp. 111–42.

Collins, Jennifer. 1994. "Religious Education Sparks Controversy." *Latinamerica Press* 26, no. 39 (October 27): 2.

Comblin, Rev. José. 1994. "Brazil: Base Communities in the Northeast." In *New Face of the Church in Latin America*, ed. Cook, pp. 202–25.

Conferencia Episcopal de Chile. 1989. "Carta a las comunidades eclesiales de base." *CELAM* (Bogotá) no. 228 (June): 1–49.

——. 1992. *Evangélicos y Sectas: Propuestas pastorales*. Santiago: CENCOSEP.

Confraternidad Evangélica Salvadoreña (CONESAL). 1987. *Estudio del crecimiento de la Iglesia Evangélica de El Salvador*. San Salvador: CONESAL.

Cook, Guillermo. 1985. *The Expectation of the Poor: Latin American Base Ecclesial Communities in Protestant Perspective*. Maryknoll, N.Y.: Orbis.

——. 1994a. "The Genesis and Practice of Protestant Base Communities in Latin America." In *New Face of the Church in Latin America*, ed. Cook, pp. 150–55.

——. 1994b. "Protestant Presence and Social Change in Latin America: Contrasting Versions." In *Coming of Age*, ed. Daniel Miller, pp. 119–41.

——. 1997. "Interchurch Relations: Exclusion, Ecumenism, and the Poor." In *Power, Politics, and Pentecostals in Latin America*, ed. Cleary and Stewart-Gambino, pp. 77–96.

Cook, Guillermo, ed. 1994. *New Face of the Church in Latin America.* Maryknoll, N.Y.: Orbis.

Coppola, Marcos. 1992. "Protests Greet New Argentine Education Law." *Latinamerica Press* 24, no. 32 (September 3): 4.

Cosgrove, Wes. 1993a. "Venezuelan Elections Reflect Discontent." *Latinamerica Press* 25, no. 2 (January 28): 4.

———. 1993b. "CELAM Returns Focus to the Grassroots." *Latinamerica Press,* 25, no. 12 (April 8): 1.

"Costa Rica." 1993. *Latinamerica Press* 25, no. 33 (September 16): 8.

Crahan, Margaret E. 1982. "International Aspects of the Role of the Catholic Church in Central America." In *Central America: International Dimensions of the Crisis,* ed. Richard E. Feinberg, New York: Holmes and Meier, pp. 213–35.

———. 1984. "The Central American Church and Regime Transformation: Attitudes and Options." In *Political Change in Central America: Internal and External Dimensions.* ed. W. Grabendorff and H. Krumiede, Boulder, Colo.: Westview Press, pp. 139–52.

———. 1991. "Church and State in Latin America: Assassinating Some Old and New Stereotypes." *Daedalus* 20, no. 3 (summer): 131–58.

———. 1992. "Religion, Revolution, and Counterrevolution: The Role of the Religious Right in Central America." In *The Right and Democracy in Latin America,* ed. Douglas A. Chalmers, Maria do Carmo Campello de Souza, and Atilio A. Boron, New York: Praeger, pp. 163–82.

Damen, Franz. 1987. "Las sectas: avalancha o desafío? *Cuarto Intermedio* (Cochabamba, Bolivia), no. 3 (May).

Daudelin, Jean and W. E. Hewitt. 1995. "Latin American Politics: Exit the Catholic Church?" In *Organized Religion in the Political Transformation of Latin America,* ed. Pattnayak, pp. 177–94.

Deiros, Pablo A. 1991. "Protestant Fundamentalism in Latin America." In *Fundamentalisms Observed,* ed. Marty and Appleby, pp. 142–96.

Deiros, Pablo A., ed. 1986. *Los evangélicos y el poder político en América Latina.* Grand Rapids, Mich.: William B. Eerdmans.

De Powell, Elsa R., et al. 1992. "Evangelical Involvement in the Political Life of Latin America." *Transformation* 9, no. 3: 8–14.

Diamond, Sara. 1989. *Spiritual Warfare: The Politics of the Christian Right.* Boston: South End Press.

Dodson, Michael. 1979. "The Christian Left in Latin American Politics." *Journal of Interamerican Studies and World Affairs* 21, no. 1: 45–68.

———. 1986. "Nicaragua: The Struggle for the Church." In *Religion and Political Conflict in Latin America,* ed. Levine, pp. 79–105.

———. 1997. "Pentecostals, Politics, and Public Space in Latin America." In *Power, Politics, and Pentecostals in Latin America,* ed. Cleary and Stewart-Gambino, pp. 25–40.

Dodson, Michael, and Laura O'Shaugnessy. 1990. *Nicaragua's Other Revolution: Religious Faith and Political Struggle.* Chapel Hill, N.C.: University of North Carolina Press.

Domínguez, Jorge I. 1989. "International and National Aspects of the Catholic Church in Cuba." *Cuban Studies* 19: 43–60.

Drogus, Carol Ann. 1992. "Popular Movements and the Limits of Political Mobilization at the Grassroots in Brazil." In *Conflict and Competition,* ed. Cleary and Stewart-Gambino, pp. 63–86.

———. 1997. "Private Power and Public Power: Pentecostalism, Base Communities, and Gender." In *Power, Politics, and Pentecostals in Latin America,* ed. Cleary and Stewart-Gambino, 1997, pp. 55–75.

Dussel, Enrique. 1976. *History and Theology of Liberation.* Maryknoll, N.Y.: Orbis.

Dussel, Enrique, ed. 1992. *The Church in Latin America: 1492–1992.* Maryknoll, N.Y.: Orbis.

"Ecuador." 1993. *Latinamerica Press* 25, no. 15 (April 29): 8.

EFE. 1995. "Poverty, Especially Rural, Increasing in Region." *Latin American News Update* (LANU) 2, no. 3 (March): 6.

ENI. 1994. "Latin America: Religious Conflict." *Latinamerica Press* 26, no. 47 (December 22): 8.

Escobar, J. Samuel. 1994. "Promise and Precariousness of Latin American Protestantism." In *Coming of Age,* ed. Daniel Miller, pp. 3–35.

Evans, T. E. 1990. Religious Conversion in Quetzaltenango Guatemala. Ph.D. diss., University of Pittsburgh.

Fleet, Michael. 1985. *The Rise and Fall of Chilean Christian Democracy.* Princeton, N.J.: Princeton University Press.

Fleet, Michael, and Brian H. Smith. 1997. *The Catholic Church and Democracy in Chile and Peru.* Notre Dame, Ind.: University of Notre Dame Press.

Flora, Cornelia Butler. 1976. *Pentecostalism in Colombia: Baptism by Fire and Spirit.* Cranbury, N.J.: Associated University Presses.

Fogarty, Michael P. 1957. *Christian Democracy in Western Europe, 1820–1953.* London: Routledge and Kegan Paul.

Fontaine Talavera, Arturo, and Harald Beyer. 1991. "Retrato del movimiento evangélico a la luz de las encuestas de opinión pública." *Estudios Públicos* (Santiago) 44 (spring): 63–124.

Foroohar, Manzar. 1989. *The Catholic Church and Social Change in Nicaragua.* Albany, N.Y.: State University Press of New York.

Frasca, Tim. 1989. "AIDS in Latin America: The Looming Crisis." *Latinamerica Press* 21, no. 47 (December 21): 1–2.

Freston, Paul. 1993. "Brother Votes for Brother: The New Politics of Protestantism in Brazil." In *Rethinking Protestantism in Latin America,* ed. Garrard-Burnett and Stoll, pp. 45–65.

———. 1994. "Brazil: Church Growth, Parachurch Agencies, and Politics." In *New Face of the Church in Latin America,* ed. Cook, pp. 226–42.

———. 1997. "Evangelicalism and Politics: A Comparison between Africa and Latin America." *Transformation* 14, no. 1 (January-March): 23–29.

Fried, Jonathan L., and Marvin Gettleman, eds. 1983. "Religion and Revolution: A Protestant Voice." In *Guatemala in Rebellion: Unfinished History,* ed. Fried and Gettleman, New York: Grove Press.

Froehle, Bryan T. 1995. "Religious Competition, Community Building and Democracy in Latin America: Grassroots Religious Organizations in Venezuela." In *Religion and Democracy in Latin America,* ed. Swatos, pp. 27–44.

———. 1997. "Pentecostals and Evangelicals in Venezuela: Consolidating Gains, Moving in New Directions." In *Power, Politics, and Pentecostals in Latin America,* ed. Cleary and Stewart-Gambino, pp. 201–25.

Galilea W., Carmen. 1992. *Católicos carismáticos y Protestantes pentecostales: Análisis comparativo de sus vivencias religiosas.* Santiago: Centro Bellarmino—Centro de Investigaciones Sociales.

Galindo, Florencio. 1992. *El protestantismo fundamentalista: Una experiencia ambigua para América Latina.* Madrid: Editorial Verbo Divino.

Garma Navarro, Carlos. 1987. *El protestantismo en una comunidad totonaca de Puebla.* Mexico City: Instituto Nacional Indigenista.

Garrard-Burnett, Virginia. 1986. A History of Protestantism in Guatemala. Ph.D. diss., Tulane University.

———. 1989. "Protestantism in Rural Guatemala, 1872–1954." *Latin American Research Review* 24, no. 2: 127–42.

Garrard-Burnett, Virginia, and David Stoll, eds. 1993. *Rethinking Protestantism in Latin America.* Philadelphia: Temple University Press.

Gilfeather, Katherine O'Brien, M. M. 1992. *El rol de ecumenismo protestante como posible solución al impasse en las relaciones entre la iglesia católica y la comunidad pentecostal.* Santiago: Centro Bellarmino—Centro de Investigaciones Sociales.

Gill, Anthony J. 1994. "Rendering to Caesar? Religious Competition and Catholic Political Strategy in Latin America, 1962–1979." *American Journal of Political Science* 38, no. 2 (May): 403–25.

Gill, Lesley. 1993. "Religious Mobility and the Many Words of God in La Paz, Bolivia." In *Rethinking Protestantism in Latin America,* ed. Garrard-Burnett and Stoll, pp. 180–98.

Gismondi, Michael. 1986. "Transformations of the Holy." *Latin American Perspectives* 13, no. 3.

Goffin, Alvin M. 1994. *The Rise of Protestant Evangelism in Ecuador, 1895–1990.* Gainesville, Fla.: University Press of Florida.

Goldin, Liliana R., and Brent Metz. 1991. "An Expression of Cultural Change: Invisible Converts to Protestantism among Highland Guatemalan Mayas." *Ethnology* 30, no. 4: 325–38.

González Dorado, A. 1992. "La iglesia ante el fenómeno social de las sectas." *CHRISTUS* 42 (November/December): 50–54.

Goonan, Brian K. 1996. "The New Look of the Churches." *Latinamerica Press* 28, no. 35 (September 26): 2–3.

Greene, Anne. 1993. *The Catholic Church in Haiti: Political and Social Change.* East Lansing, Mich.: Michigan State University Press.

Greenway, Roger S. 1994. "Protestant Mission Activity in Latin America." In *Coming of Age,* ed. Daniel Miller, pp. 175–204.

Grigulevich, Josef. 1984. *La iglesia católica y el movimiento de liberación en América Latina.* Moscow: Editorial Progreso.

Gutiérrez, Gustavo. 1973. *A Theology of Liberation.* Maryknoll, N.Y.: Orbis.

Gutwirth, Jacques. 1991. "Pentecotisme national et audiovisuel a Porto Alegre, Bresil." *Archives des Sciences Sociales des Religions* 37, no. 73: 99–114.

Hallum, Anne Motley. 1996. *Beyond Missionaries: Toward an Understanding of the Protestant Movement in Central America.* Lanham, Md.: Rowman and Littlefield.

Hansen, Laurie. 1992. "Pope Strikes Out against Sects Wooing Latin American Catholics away from Church." *Catholic Herald* (Milwaukee) 122, 42 (October 22): 1, 7.

Hartz, Louis. 1955. *The Liberal Tradition in America: An Interpretation of American Political Thought since the Revolution.* New York: Harcourt Brace.

Hennelly, Alfred T., S. J., ed. 1990. *Liberation Theology: A Documentary History.* Maryknoll, N.Y.: Orbis.

———. 1993. *Santo Domingo and Beyond.* Maryknoll, N.Y.: Orbis.

Hewitt, W. E. 1991. *Base Christian Communities and Social Change in Brazil.* Lincoln, Neb.: University of Nebraska Press.

Hoekstra, Angela. 1991. "Pentecostalismo rural en Pernambuco (Brasil): Algo más que una protesta simbólica." In *Algo más que opio,* ed. Boudewijnse, Droogers, and Kamsteeg, pp. 43–56.

Hoffnagel, Judith C. 1978. The Believers: Pentecostals in a Brazilian City. Ph.D. diss., Indiana University.

Hollenweger, Walter J. 1986. "After Twenty Years' Research on Pentecostalism." *International Review of Mission* 75, 297.

Huntington, Deborah, and Enrique Domínguez. 1984. "The Salvation Brokers: Evangelicals in Central America." *NACLA Report on the Americas* 18, no. 1 (January/February): 2–36.

Idígoras, José Luis, S. J. 1991. *La religión fenómeno popular.* Lima: Ediciones Paulinas.

IPS. 1995. "The Bishops versus the Market." *Latinamerica Press* 27, no. 18 (May 18): 2.

———. 1997. "Illegal Abortions Are Major Health Problem." *Latinamerica Press* 29, no. 22 (June 12): 4–5.

Ireland, Rowan. 1991. *Kingdoms Come: Religion and Politics in Brazil*. Pittsburgh, Pa.: University of Pittsburgh Press.

Jeffrey, Paul. 1995. "Guatemala: Bishops Record Violent History." *Latinamerica Press* 27, no. 17 (May 11): 8.

———. 1996a. "Market Sets the Mood for Churches." *Latinamerica Press* 28, no. 35 (September 26): 6–7.

———. 1996b. "Catholics Side with Persecuted Evangelicals." *Latinamerica Press* 38, no. 47 (December 19): 2.

———. 1997. "Religious Tensions Rise over School Books." *Latinamerica Press* 29, no. 16 (May 1): 3.

Kamsteeg, Frans. 1991. "Pastor y discípulo: El rol de lideres y laicos en el crecimiento de las iglesias pentecostales en Arequipa, Perú." In *Algo más que opio,* ed. Boudewijnse, Droogers, and Kamsteeg, pp. 95–113.

Kanagy, Conrad L. 1995. "The Formation and Development of a Protestant Conversion Movement among the Highland Quichua of Ecuador." In *Religion and Democracy in Latin America,* ed. Swatos, pp. 135–47.

Kessler, John. 1992. *500 años de evangelización en América Latina desde una perspectiva evangélica.* San José, Costa Rica: Departamento de Publicaciones del Instituto Internacional de Evangelización a Fondo.

Kirk, John M. 1989. *Between God and the Party: Religion and Politics in Revolutionary Cuba.* Tampa, Fla.: University of South Florida Press.

Lagos S., Humberto. 1982. *La función de las minorías religiosas: Las transacciones del Protestantismo chileno en el período 1973–1981 del gobierno militar.* Louvain la Nueve: n.p.

Lagos S., Humberto, and Arturo Chacón Herrera. 1987. *Los evangélicos en Chile: Una lectura sociológica.* Concepción: Ediciones Literatura Americana Reunida.

Lalive d'Epinay, Christian. 1969. *Haven of the Masses: A Study of the Pentecostal Movement in Chile.* London: Lutterworth.

———. 1974. "Les religions au Chile entre l'alienation et la prise de conscience." *Social Compass* (Brussels) 21: 85–100.

———. 1975. *Religion, dynamique sociale et dépendance: Les mouvements protestants en Argentine et au Chili.* Paris: Mouton.

———. 1983. "Political Regimes and Millenarianism in a Dependent Society: Reflections on Pentecostalism in Chile." *Concilium* no. 161: 42–54.

Langton, Kenneth P. 1986. "The Church, Social Consciousness, and Protest?" *Comparative Political Studies* 19, no. 3 (October).

Langton, Kenneth P., and Ronald Rapoport. 1976. "Religion and Leftist Mobilization in Chile." *Comparative Political Studies* 9, no. 3: 277–308.

"Latin America." 1994. *Latinamerica Press* 26, no. 14 (April 21): 8.

Latin American Episcopal Council (CELAM). 1970. *The Church in the Present-Day Transformation of Latin America in Light of the Council.* 2 vols. Bogotá: General Secretariat of CELAM.

———. 1979. "Evangelization in Latin America's Present and Future." In *Puebla and Beyond,* ed. John Eagleson and Philip Scharper, Maryknoll, N.Y.: Orbis, pp. 113–285.

Latourette, Kenneth Scott. 1961. "Latin America." In *Christianity in a Revolutionary Age: A History of Christianity in the Nineteenth and Twentieth Centuries,* vol. 3, ed. Latourette, 5 vols., New York: Harper, 1958–1962, pp. 284–352.

———. 1962. "Contrasting Developments in Burgeoning Latin America." In *Christianity in a Revolutionary Age: A History of Christianity in the Nineteenth and Twentieth Centuries,* vol. 5, ed. Latourette, 5 vols., New York: Harper, 1958–1962, pp. 158–240.

Lee, Gerry G. 1992. "Venezuelan Church Takes on New Role." *Latinamerica Press* 24, no. 29 (August 13): 1–2.

Lernoux, Penny. 1980. *Cry of the People.* New York: Doubleday.

———. 1989. *People of God: The Struggle for World Catholicism.* New York: Viking Press.

Levine, Daniel. 1981. *Religion and Politics in Latin America: The Catholic Church in Venezuela and Colombia.* Princeton, N.J.: Princeton University Press.

———. 1992. *Popular Voices in Latin American Catholicism.* Princeton, N.J.: Princeton University Press.

———. 1995. "Protestants and Catholics in Latin America: A Family Portrait." In *Fundamentalisms Comprehended,* ed. Marty and Appleby, pp. 155–78.

Levine, Daniel, ed. 1980. *Churches and Politics in Latin America.* Beverly Hills, Calif.: Sage Publications.

———. 1986. *Religion and Political Conflict in Latin America.* Chapel Hill, N.C.: University of North Carolina Press.

Lipset, Seymour M. 1960. *Political Man.* Garden City, N.Y.: Doubleday.

Lynch, Colum. 1989. "Catholics, Evangelicals Tangle amid Latin American Turmoil." *San Francisco Chronicle,* May 10, p. 4.

Mainwaring, Scott. 1986. *The Catholic Church and Politics in Brazil, 1916–1985.* Stanford, Calif.: Stanford University Press.

———. 1989. "Grass-roots Catholic Groups and Politics in Brazil." In

The Progressive Church in Latin America, ed. Mainwaring and Wilde, pp. 151–92.

Mainwaring, Scott, and Alexander Wilde, eds. 1989. *The Progressive Church in Latin America.* Notre Dame, Ind.: University of Notre Dame Press.

Marcom, John, Jr. 1990. "The Fire Down South." *Forbes Magazine* 146, no. 8 (October 15): 56, 57, 64, 66, 71.

McCoy, John. 1989. "Robbing Peter to Pay Paul: The Evangelical Tide." *Latinamerica Press* 21, no. 24 (June 29): 1, 8.

McGovern, Arthur F., S. J. 1989. *Liberation Theology and Its Critics.* Maryknoll, N.Y.: Orbis.

McPhaul, John. 1991. "Church Raps Costa Rica Sex Education." *Latinamerica Press* 23, no. 45 (December 5): 7.

Mariz, Cecília. 1994a. *Coping with Poverty: Pentecostals and Christian Base Communities in Brazil.* Philadelphia, Pa.: Temple University Press.

———. 1994b. "Religion and Poverty in Brazil." In *New Face of the Church in Latin America,* ed. Cook, pp. 75–81.

Martin, David. 1990. *Tongues of Fire: The Explosion of Protestantism in Latin America.* Oxford, UK: Blackwell.

———. 1996. *Forbidden Revolutions: Pentecostalism in Latin America, Catholicism in Eastern Europe.* London: SPCK.

Martins, José Pedro. 1989. "Brazil: Diverse Social Organizations Are at the Forefront of the Struggle." *Latinamerica Press* 21, no. 47 (December 21): 5.

———. 1990. "Brazil: Conservative Church Gains Strength." *Latinamerica Press* 22, no. 32 (September 6): 1–2.

Marty, Martin E., and R. Scott Appleby, eds. 1991. *Fundamentalisms Observed.* Chicago: University of Chicago Press.

———. 1993. *Fundamentalisms and Society: Reclaiming the Sciences, the Family and Education.* Chicago: University of Chicago Press.

———. 1995. *Fundamentalisms Comprehended.* Chicago: University of Chicago Press.

Marzal, Manuel M. 1989. *Los caminos religiosos de los inmigrantes en la Gran Lima: El caso de El Augustino.* Lima: Fondo Editorial, Pontífica Universidad Católica del Perú.

Mecham, J. Lloyd. 1966. *Church and State in Latin America: A History of Politico-Ecclesiastical Relations.* 2d ed. Chapel Hill, N.C.: University of North Carolina Press.

Meehan, Maureen. 1991. "Annulment Used as Divorce Loophole in Chile." *Latinamerica Press* 23 (July 11): 4.

Merino, Denis. 1990. "Peru: Religious Tensions Dominate Election." *Latinamerica Press* 22, no. 20 (May 31): 1–2.

Merrill, Collett. 1987. "The Cross and the Flag." *Progressive* (December): 18–20.

Miller, Daniel R., ed. 1994. *Coming of Age: Protestantism in Contemporary Latin America*. Lanham, Md.: University Press of America.

Miller, Dave. 1992. "Church-State Separation in Bolivia." *Latinamerica Press*, 24, no. 2 (January 23): 7.

Miranda, José. 1974. *Marx and the Bible*. Maryknoll, N.Y.: Orbis.

Montgomery, Tommie Sue. 1980. "Latin American Evangelicals: Oaxtepec and Beyond." In *Churches and Politics in Latin America*, ed. Levine, pp. 87–107.

Morley, Samuel A. 1995. *Poverty and Inequality in Latin America: The Impact of Adjustment and Recovery in the 1980s*. Baltimore: Johns Hopkins University Press.

Mutchler, David E. 1971. *The Church as a Political Factor in Latin America*. New York: Praeger.

Novaes, Regina. 1985. *Os escolhidos de Deus: Pentecostais, trabalhadores e Ciudadania*. Cadernos de ISER, no. 19. Rio de Janeiro: Instituto Superior de Estudos da Religião (ISER).

Novak, Michael. 1982. "Why Latin America Is Poor." *Atlantic Monthly* (March): 66–75.

Nuñez, Emilio A., and William D. Taylor. 1989. *Crisis in Latin America: An Evangelical Perspective*. Chicago: Moody Press.

Padilla, C. René. 1994. "New Actors on the Political Scene in Latin America." In *New Face of the Church in Latin America*, ed. Cook, pp. 82–95.

Palma, Samuel, and Hugo Villela. 1990. "Die Pfingstbegung als Volksreligion de lateinamerikanischen Protestantismus: Einige Elemente zum Verstandnis der Dynamic der Pfingstkirchen in Lateinamerika." *Zeitschrift für Mission* 16, 1.

"Paraguay." 1993. *Latinamerica Press* 25, no. 35 (September 30): 8.

Pattnayak, Satya R., ed. 1995. *Organized Religion in the Political Transformation of Latin America*. Lanhan, Md.: University Press of America.

Peck, Jane Cary. 1984. "Reflections from Costa Rica on Protestantism's Dependence and Nonliberative Social Function." *Journal of Ecumenical Studies* 21, no. 2: 181–98.

Peerman, Dean. 1993. "CELAM IV: Maneuvering and Marking Time in Santo Domingo." *Christian Century* (February 17): 180–85.

"Peru." 1993. *Latinamerica Press* 25, no. 28 (July 29): 8.

Petersen, Douglas. 1997. "Towards a Latin American Pentecostal Political Praxis." *Transformation* 14, no. 1 (January-March): 30–32.

Peterson, Anna L. 1997. *Martyrdom and the Politics of Religion: Progressive Catholicism in El Salvador's Civil War*. Albany, N.Y.: State University of New York Press.

Plou, Dafne Sabanes. 1990. "Argentina: Abortion Issue Provokes Debate." *Latinamerica Press* 22, no. 35 (September 27): 5.

——. 1991. "Churches Vie for Latin Souls." *Latinamerica Press* 23 (February 14): 7.

——. 1992. "Argentine Churches Unite for Change." *Latinamerica Press* 24, no. 31 (August 27): 7.

——. 1994. "Menem Ignites Abortion Debate in Argentina." *Latinamerica Press* 26, no. 28 (July 28): 1.

——. 1996. "Building Ecumenical Bridges." *Latinamerica Press* 28, no. 35 (September 26): 14.

——. 1997. "Bishops Take Stand against Government." *Latinamerica Press* 29, no. 23 (June 19): 3.

Poblete, Renato, S. J., and Carmen Galilea W. 1984. *Movimiento pentecostal y Iglesia católica en medios populares.* Santiago: Centro Bellarmino.

Puentes Oliva, Pedro. 1975. *Posición evangélica.* Santiago: Editora Nacional Gabriela Mistral.

Rayo, Gustavo, and William Porath. 1990. *Perfil y opciones sociales de los católicos chilenos.* Santiago: Centro de Estudios de la Realidad Contemporanea (CERC).

Richard, Pablo. 1992. "La iglesia católica después de Santo Domingo." *Pastoral Popular* (Santiago): 43, nos. 224/25 (November/December): 14–22.

Roberts, Bryan. 1968. "Protestant Groups and Coping with Urban Life in Guatemala." *American Journal of Sociology* 73: 753–67.

Rocha, Guilherme Salgado. 1994. "Brazilian Church Creates TV Network." *Latinamerica Press* 26, no. 15 (April 28): 4.

——. 1995. "The Fight for Land Goes On." *Latinamerica Press* 27, no. 3 (February 2): 6.

Rohter, Larry. 1994a. "Liberal Wing of Haiti's Catholic Church Resists Military." *New York Times,* July 24, p. Y3.

——. 1994b. "Over Cheers for Aristide, Silence of Haiti's Bishops." *New York Times,* September 28, pp. A1, A7.

——. 1998. "Pope Asks Cubans to Seek New Path toward Freedom." *New York Times,* January 26, pp. A1, A8.

Rolim, Francisco C. 1985. *Pentecostais no Brasil: Uma interpretação socio-religiosa.* Petropolis, Brazil: Vozes.

——. 1994. *Pentecostalismo: Brasil e América Latina.* Petropolis, Brazil: Vozes.

Rose, Susan, and Quentin Schultze. 1993. "The Evangelical Awakening in Guatemala: Fundamentalist Impact on Education and Media." In *Fundamentalisms and Society,* ed. Marty and Appleby, pp. 415–51.

Ross, John. 1994. "Chiapas Uprising Rocks Mexican Church." *Latinamerica Press* 26, no. 2 (January 27): 1–2.

——. 1996. "The Changing Catholic Church." *Latinamerica Press* 28, no. 35 (September 26): 12–13.

Rycroft, W. Stanley. 1958. *Religion and Faith in Latin America.* Philadelphia: Westminster Press.

Ryser, Jeffrey, et al. 1990. "Latin America's Protestants: A Potential New Force for Change." *Business Week,* no. 3162 (June 4): 79.

Saenz, Adolfo Miranda. 1994. "Nicaragua: Political Metamorphosis of Evangelicals." In *New Face of the Church in Latin America,* ed. Cook, pp. 190–201.

Samandú, Luis, ed. 1991. *Protestantismos y procesos sociales in Centroamérica.* San José, Costa Rica: EDUCA.

Schafer, Heinrich. 1992. *Protestantismo y crisis social en América Central.* San José, Costa Rica: Departamento Ecuménico de Investigaciones (DEI).

Segundo, Juan Luis, S.J. 1973. *A Theology for Artisans of a New Humanity.* 5 vols. Maryknoll, N.Y.: Orbis.

Seligson, Mitchell A. and Joel M. Jutkowitz. 1994. *Guatemalan Values and the Prospects for Democratic Development.* Pittsburgh: Development Associates/University of Pittsburgh/Asociación de Investigación y Estudios Sociales (ASIES).

Sepúlveda, Juan. 1994. "The Pentecostal Movement in Latin America." In *New Face of the Church in Latin America,* ed. Cook, pp. 68–74.

Serbin, Ken. 1992. "Latin America's Catholics: Postliberationism?" *Christianity and Crisis* (December 14): 403–407.

——. 1997. "Churches, Religious Pluralism, and Politics in Brazil on the Eve of the Third Millennium." Paper presented at the XXI International Congress of the Latin American Studies Association, Guadalajara, Mexico, April 17–19.

Sexton, James D. 1978. "Protestantism and Modernization in Two Guatemalan Towns." *American Ethnologist* 5, no. 2: 280–302.

Shaull, Richard. 1996. "Reflections on Pentecostalism." *Latinamerica Press* 28, no. 35 (September 26): 11.

Sigmund, Paul E. 1990. *Liberation Theology at the Crossroads: Democracy or Revolution?* New York: Oxford University Press.

Sigmund, Paul E., ed. 1998. *Evangelization and Religious Freedom in Latin America.* Maryknoll, N.Y.: Orbis.

Simons, Marlise. 1982. "Latin America's New Gospel." *New York Times Magazine,* November 7, pp. 45–47ff.

——. 1988. "Abortions across Latin America Rising Despite Illegality and Risks." *New York Times,* November 26, pp. 1, 4.

Smith, Brian H. 1979. "Churches and Human Rights in Latin America: Recent Trends in the Subcontinent." *Journal of Interamerican Studies and World Affairs* 21, no. 1: 89–128.

——. 1982. *The Church and Politics in Chile: Challenges to Modern Catholicism.* Princeton, N.J.: Princeton University Press.

———. 1990. *More Than Altruism: The Politics of Private Foreign Aid.* Princeton, N.J.: Princeton University Press.

———. 1998. "Nonprofit Organizations in International Development: Agents of Empowerment or Preservers of Stability? In *Private Action and the Public Good*, ed. Walter W. Powell and Elisabeth Clemens, New Haven, Conn.: Yale University Press.

Smith, Christian. 1991. *The Emergence of Liberation Theology: Radical Religion and Social Movement Theory.* Chicago: University of Chicago Press.

———. 1995. "The Spirit of Democracy: Base Communities, Protestantism, and Democratization in Latin America." In *Religion and Democracy in Latin America*, ed. Swatos, pp. 1–21.

———. 1997. "Revolutionary Evangelicals in Nicaragua: Political Opportunity, Class Interests, and Religious Identity." *Journal for the Scientific Study of Religion* 36 (September): 440–54.

Smith, Christian, ed. 1996. *Disruptive Religion: The Force of Faith in Social Movement Activism.* New York: Routledge.

Spykman, Gordon, et al. 1988. *Let My People Live: Faith and Struggle in Central America.* Grand Rapids, Mich.: William B. Eerdmans.

Steigenga, Timothy J. 1994. "Protestantism, the State and Society in Guatemala." In *Coming of Age*, ed. Daniel Miller, pp. 143–72.

———. 1995. "Protestantism and Politics in Costa Rica: The Religious Determinants of Political Activities and Beliefs." Paper presented at the 53rd annual meeting of the Midwest Political Science Association, Chicago, April 6–8.

Steigenga, Timothy J., and Kenneth M. Coleman. 1995. "Protestant Political Orientations and the Structure of Political Opportunity: Chile, 1972–1991." *Polity* 27, no. 3 (spring): 465–82.

Stein, Andrew J. 1992. "Religion and Mass Politics in Central America." Paper presented at the annual meeting of the New England Council of Latin American Studies, Boston University, October 24.

———. 1994. "Religion, Ethnicity and Politics in Guatemala." Paper presented at the XVIII International Congress of the Latin American Studies Association, Atlanta, March 9–12.

———. 1995. The Prophetic Mission, the Catholic Church and Politics: Nicaragua in the Context of Central America. Ph.D. diss., University of Pittsburgh.

———. 1997a. "The Church." In *Nicaragua without Illusions*, ed. Thomas W. Walker, Wilmington, Del.: Scholarly Resources, Inc., pp. 235–47.

———. 1997b. "La labor pastoral y la opción preferencial por los pobres en la Iglesia Católica de Nicaragua." Paper presented at the XXI International Congress of the Latin American Studies Association, Guadalajara, Mexico, April 17–19.

———. 1998. "The Consequences of the Nicaraguan Revolution for Political Tolerance: Explaining Differences among the Mass Public, Catholic Priests and Secular Elites." *Comparative Politics,* 30, 3 (April): 335–53.

Stewart-Gambino, Hannah. 1992. "Introduction: New Game, New Rules." In *Conflict and Competition,* ed. Cleary and Stewart-Gambino, pp. 1–19.

———. 1994. "Church and State in Latin America." *Current History* 93, no. 581 (March): 129–33.

Stoll, David. 1990. *Is Latin America Turning Protestant? The Politics of Evangelical Growth.* Berkeley, Calif.: University of California Press.

———. 1993. *Between Two Armies in the Ixil Towns of Guatemala.* New York: Columbia University Press.

Swatos, William H., Jr., ed. 1995. *Religion and Democracy in Latin America.* New Brunswick, N.J.: Transaction Books.

Tapia, Andres. 1995. "Postcard from Peru." *Christianity Today,* June 19, pp. 24–26.

Tautz, Carlos. 1995. "Religious Sparks Fly in Brazil." *Latinamerica Press* 27, no. 89 (October 26): 1, 8.

———. 1996. "TV Is New Tool in 'Soul War.'" *Latinamerica Press* 28, no. 35 (September 26): 10.

———. 1997. "Bishops Criticize Shocking Inequality." *Latinamerica Press* 29, no. 15 (April 24): 4–5.

Tennekes, Juan. 1978. "Le mouvement pentecotiste chilien et la politique." *Social Compass* 25, no. 1: 55–79.

Thiemann, Ronald F. 1996. *Religion in Public Life: A Dilemma for Democracy.* Washington, D.C.: Georgetown University Press.

Treaster, Joseph B. 1988a. "Balm for a Bruised Clergy, and Hope for Believers." *New York Times,* April 28, p. 4.

———. 1988b. "Castro Suggests Freeing Hundreds." *New York Times,* May 22, p. 3.

———. 1989. "Curbs Easing, Cuba Expects a Papal Visit." *New York Times,* Feb. 12, p. 9.

Valcarcel, Luis E. 1972 (1928). *Tempestad en los Andes.* 2nd ed. Lima: Editorial Universo.

Valverde, Jaime. 1990. *Las sectas en Costa Rica.* San José, Costa Rica: Editorial Departamento Ecuménico de Investigaciones (DEI).

Walsh, Michael, and Brian Davies, eds. 1991. *Proclaiming Justice and Peace: Papal Documents from 'Rerum Novarum' through 'Centesimus Annus.'* Mystic, Conn.: Twenty-third Publications.

Westmeier, Karl-Wilhelm. 1986. *Reconciling Heaven and Earth: The Transcendent Enthusiasm and Growth of an Urban Protestant Community, Bogotá, Colombia.* New York: Peter Lang.

———. 1993. "Themes of Pentecostal Expansion in Latin America." *International Bulletin of Missionary Research* 17, no. 2 (April): 72–78.

Westropp, Mary. 1983. "Christian Counterinsurgency." *Cultural Survival Quarterly* 7, no. 3: 28–31.

WFS. 1994. "What's Happening to the Peruvian Family?" *Latinamerica Press* 26, no. 38 (October 20): 5.

Willems, Emilio. 1967. *Followers of the New Faith: Culture Change and the Rise of Protestantism in Brazil and Chile.* Nashville, Tenn.: Vanderbilt University Press.

Williams, Philip J. 1997. "The Sound of Tambourines: The Politics of Pentecostal Growth in El Salvador." In *Power, Politics, and Pentecostals in Latin American,* ed. Cleary and Stewart-Gambino, pp. 179–200.

Wilson, Everett A. 1983. "Sanguine Saints: Pentecostalism in El Salvador." *Church History* 52, no. 2: 186–98.

———. 1994a. "The Dynamics of Latin American Pentecostalism." In *Coming of Age,* ed. Daniel Miller, pp. 89–116.

———. 1994b. "Latin American Pentecostalism: Challenging the Stereotypes of Pentecostal Passivity." *Transformation* 11, no. 1 (January-March): 19–24.

———. 1997. "Guatemalan Pentecostals: Something of Their Own." In *Power, Politics and Pentecostals in Latin America,* ed. Cleary and Stewart-Gambino, pp. 139–62.

Winn, Peter. 1992. *Americas: The Changing Face of Latin America and the Caribbean.* New York: Pantheon Books.

Zub, Roberto K. 1993. *Protestantismo y elecciones en Nicaragua.* Managua: Ediciones Nicarao.

———. 1994. "Relaciones iglesia y estado en Nicaragua: Una perspectiva protestante." Unpublished paper, August.

———. 1996. "Rol de la iglesia y religión en las elecciones 96 en Nicaragua." Unpublished paper, November.

INDEX

AIDS (HIV), 44, 52, 59, 81, 92, 95
abortion, 44–45, 48, 52, 57–58, 80–82, 92–93, 95, 98
Argentina: Catholicism in, 9, 52, 58, 61–62, 95, 103n. 2; divorce reform in, 103n. 2; Pentecostalism in, 36, 95
Assemblies of God, 21, 25, 37–38, 44

base communities (*comunidades eclesiales de base,* also CEBs), 9–10, 12–15, 17, 29, 38–39, 44, 57, 63, 65, 67–79, 82, 86, 89, 104n. 5
birth control. *See* contraception
bishops (in Latin America): mediators of political conflict, 51–52, 89; statements about Protestantism, 4; support for democracy, 52, 54, 60; support for family values / sexual morality, 52, 56–60; support for human rights, 52–54, 60; support for social justice, 51–56, 60; tension with government leaders, 56. *See also* Catholicism
Bolivia: Catholicism in, 60–61; constitution of, 60; Pentecostalism in, 43, 60, 93
Brasil para Cristo, 37
Brazil: Catholicism in, 12, 29, 52, 56, 58, 63–64, 66, 68–69, 71, 77–78, 80–81, 92–93, 104n. 5; Pentecostalism in, 25, 36–38, 42–46, 87, 92–93; Protestantism in, 2, 36
Brazilian Evangelical Association (AEVB), 46, 102n. 1
Brazilian Protestant Federation, 37
Boff, Leonardo, O.F.M., 12

Campus Crusade for Christ, 22–23
Cardoso, Fernando Henrique, 56
Catholic Relief Services (CRS), 23–24, 65

Catholicism (in Latin America): and AIDS, 59, 81; Charismatic Movement in, 46, 64, 69–70, 76; conservative tendencies in, 12–13, 46, 51, 56, 79, 86–88, 101n. 4; divisions in, 1, 11, 14, 79–83, 97–98, 101–2n. 5; government financial support for, 44–45; as incentive for economic advancement, 29–30; interactions with Pentecostalism, 15–19, 60–64, 85–99; lack of clergy and religious in, 7; lack of spirituality in, 7–8, 78; legal privileges of, 44, 49, 52, 60–64, 80, 92, 94; links to foreign support, 23–24, 103n. 3; and Marxism, 11, 67–68, 73, 80; as opposition force to military rule, 10–11, 36, 67, 89; papal criticisms of, 7–8, 11; political attitudes and behavior in, 47, 73–74, 89; reforms in during 1960s and 1970s, 9–10, 101n. 4; as refuge from the world, 15–17, 85–87; religious practice in, 74–76; and support for democracy, 10, 17, 71–74, 97, 99; and support for social justice, 18–19, 53, 55, 65–68, 79–80, 86, 88–90, 102n. 6; and use of the media, 63; women in, 77–78, 81. *See also* bishops, priests
CEBs. *See* base communities
CELADE III (Third Latin American Congress on Evangelization), 40–41
CELAM (Latin American Episcopal Conference), 9, 53, 54–55, 58, 62; Fourth General Assembly of, at Santo Domingo (1992), 4, 53–54, 63; Second General Assembly of, at Medellín (1968), 9, 13, 54; Third General Assembly of, at Puebla (1979), 53–54

Religious Politics in Latin America

Significant religious and cultural transformations are underway throughout Latin rica which will alter the contours of society. Brian H. Smith sheds light on these ges with a survey of the recent trends in Pentecostal and Catholic religion and politics is region.

Despite considerable efforts by the Vatican throughout the 1980s to pull the Latin rican Catholic Church back from intense social and political involvement, Catholi- is still very much a political force throughout the region. A new generation of con- tive bishops appointed by the pope has felt obligated to preach the social doctrine of Church in spite of the bishops' conservative religious ideology. They have vigorously unced new economic models for enriching a minority of the population at the cost of najority who are poor, and they have opposed anti-Catholic legislative proposals.

Regardless of these efforts by Catholic prelates to maintain government support for Church's institutions, Pentecostalism—especially among low income sectors—has grown significant rate over the past twenty years. Though traditionally reluctant to involve selves in politics, Pentecostals in recent years have become more active by supporting ng political movements and by forming new Christian parties. Pentecostal religious political leaders are pushing publicly for full separation of church and state and for the l status of all religions in law.

Because their political agenda overlaps in some areas with that of Catholics, a coali- between Catholic and Pentecostal leaders could have a real impact on public policy, that over 90 percent of the population is now affiliated with one of these two minations. Differences in the political agenda of Catholics and Pentecostals remain, ver, and could complicate public policy debate in the years ahead by short-circuiting ttempts to remove religion as a significant and sometimes divisive influence in poli- n newly constituted liberal democracies in Latin America.

N H. SMITH holds the Charles and Joan Van Zoeren Chair in Religion, Ethics and s at Ripon College and has written *More Than Altruism: The Politics of Private Foreign* 1990) and is co-author of *The Catholic Church and Democracy in Chile and Peru* e Dame Press, 1997).

NIVERSITY OF NOTRE DAME PRESS
tre Dame, IN
dpress.nd.edu

Lightning Source UK Ltd.
Milton Keynes UK
UKHW021816141222
413932UK00013B/654